JEFFREY D. SACHS

A NEW
FOREIGN
POLICY

BEYOND AMERICAN
EXCEPTIONALISM

Columbia University Press
New York

Columbia University Press
Publishers Since 1893
New York   Chichester, West Sussex
cup.columbia.edu

Copyright © 2018 Jeffrey D. Sachs
All rights reserved
Library of Congress Cataloging-in-Publication Data
Names: Sachs, Jeffrey, author.
Title: A new foreign policy : beyond American exceptionalism /
Jeffrey D. Sachs.
Description: New York : Columbia University Press, 2018. |
Includes bibliographical references and index.
Identifiers: LCCN 2018006069 (print) |
LCCN 2018012223 (ebook) | ISBN 9780231547888 (electronic) |
ISBN 9780231188487 (cloth : alk. paper)
Subjects: LCSH: United States—Foreign relations—21st century. |
Exceptionalism—United States. | International economic relations. |
International cooperation.
Classification: LCC JZ1480 (ebook) | LCC JZ1480 .S23 2018 (print) |
DDC 327.73—dc23
LC record available at https://lccn.loc.gov/2018006069

Columbia University Press books are printed on permanent
and durable acid-free paper.
Printed in the United States of America

Cover design: Lisa Hamm

In memory of my mother,
Joan Barbara Sachs,
who loved peace

CONTENTS

CONTENTS

PREFACE

T he United States is failing to secure the benefits of affluence and rising global prosperity. At home, the United
States is rich—with a per capita income of around
$60,000—and getting richer. Globally, the United States is
part of a world economy that is advancing rapidly in income,
technology, and education. This should be a time of confidence and rising well-being for Americans, yet instead it is a
time of disarray, division, and unhappiness. A large majority
of Americans feel that the country is moving in the wrong
direction—and they are correct.

In domestic politics, the United States is squandering its
affluence as the super-rich relentlessly pursue more wealth at
any cost. Meeting the needs of the poor, modernizing infrastructure, and protecting the environment are put aside in
favor of cutting taxes for the rich, slashing public investments,
and eliminating environmental regulations. The United States
gets richer and unhappier at the same time, with devastating
damages from climate change, falling life expectancy, soaring
public debts, and rising political polarization.

In foreign policy, the situation is no better, as the United
States is rapidly losing its global influence. The United States

under Donald Trump is making enemies in nearly all parts of the world, even among traditional allies in Canada and the European Union, as well as with China, Russia, Iran, and countless others. "America First" is a provocation for the rest of the world, replete with American threats of trade wars, broken promises, and unilateral actions by the United States thwarting hard-won international agreements. Tensions are high and rising.

Trump's provocations are a reckless extension of a long-standing and dangerous mindset of American exceptionalism. Even when America was helping to set the global rules of trade, finance, and diplomacy after World War II, American leaders held the view that America was different, ultimately exceptional, with the inherent right to make and break the international rules of the game. The dark side of American foreign policy has long been the resort to regime change and unilateral wars, not sanctioned by the United Nations and opposed by much of global and U.S. public opinion. Trump manipulates the long-standing sense of exceptionalism, and links it to wildly exaggerated grievances against the rest of the world.

In my recent book, *Building the New American Economy*, I discussed a better way for U.S. economic management, focusing on investment-led growth oriented around the challenge of sustainable development. Sustainable development means an economy that is not only rich but also socially inclusive and environmentally sustainable. The United States achieves only one-third of the sustainable development agenda—wealth—while ignoring or even scorning the social and environmental objectives. While I had a fleeting hope that "Trump the Builder" would at least invest in American infrastructure, it is now clear that Trump will invest only in Trump and in added wealth for the richest Americans. Nonetheless, the need for sustainable development will only grow over time, and will ultimately, I believe, set the agenda in the post-Trump era.

This current volume is a companion study to the economics volume, focusing on the urgent need to revamp American foreign policy. Its theme is the same: the challenges of sustainable development (including global cooperation to head off dangerous human-induced climate change) should guide and define U.S. foreign policy in the coming generation. The exceptionalist mindset is especially dangerous today. America is part of a world with shared challenges needing shared solutions. In any event, America's power—economic, military, and technological—is far less "exceptional" than Trump and other foreign policy leaders may believe.

I recognize that the arguments in this volume may not sit well with many Americans, who have long been told that America is the sole superpower with the ability to impose its will on the rest of the world. Americans have long debated whether America should be the world's policeman, mostly taking it for granted that America can serve as such if it likes. This volume argues otherwise: that it does not make sense for America to go it alone, and that in any event, American power is far too limited to take on the rest of the world in a fit of Trumpian pique. Most importantly, the world shares a vital and urgent common interest in sustainable development. We will all lose unless we maintain the peace and the cooperation needed to end human-caused climate change, loss of biodiversity, massive pollution of the air, water, and land, and the growing inequalities of wealth, income, and power.

We live in a world of rapid technological advance. If we choose right, and harness our hard-won know-how, we can accomplish great things in our time: ending poverty, stabilizing the climate, and improving the quality of lives for billions of people including, of course, the American people. This book is offered in the hope that it will make a contribution toward a wiser, more peaceful, and more prudent American role in the world.

A NEW FOREIGN POLICY

INTRODUCTION

The American Century began in 1941.[1] It is ending now. While the United States remains the world's military giant and an economic powerhouse, America no longer dominates geopolitics or the world economy. Its military can defend the United States against attack but cannot decisively determine the direction of geopolitics, or even local politics in places where it intervenes. The key task of American foreign policy, as I see it, is to work with other nations to foster a multipolar world that is peaceful, prosperous, fair, and environmentally sustainable. America's current policies work directly against these goals. A new foreign policy is a tall order that requires a fundamental and realistic rethinking of our world and America's place in it.

The United States has long viewed itself as an exceptional nation, even as God's New Israel chosen to redeem the world.[2] This view has bipartisan support and deep roots in the country's history, culture, and religious traditions. Recent paeans to American exceptionalism include Ronald Reagan's description of the United States as "the shining city on the hill" and Madeleine Albright's as the "indispensable nation." Reagan was harking back to the Puritan leader Jonathan Winthrop, who quoted Jesus (Matthew 5:14) in declaring the colonial settlement as "a city upon the hill," with the world's eyes upon it. American exceptionalism has been called the nation's civic religion, cast in secular terms with a religious aura, as in Lincoln's invocation of America as "the last best hope of Earth."

One part of American exceptionalism is relentless war. Noting more than 280 "military interventions and nuclear standoffs on every corner of the globe," plus twenty-nine wars with the country's indigenous peoples, historian Harry S. Stout declares, "The norm of American national life is war." Part of the exceptionalist tradition has been to find divine purpose in war—to place "America's faith in the institution of war as a divine instrument and sacred mandate to be exercised around the world."[3]

In this book, I will argue that American exceptionalism is profoundly and dangerously anachronistic. Americans have believed in the righteousness of their cause in part because of the repeated military triumphs throughout history. Not only has war been justified in God's name, but also victory has been interpreted as God's providential backing of the United States. Yet this kind of exceptionalism is especially misguided in the twenty-first century. The United States lacks the relative economic and military power, not to mention the knowledge and prudence, to redeem the world through American-led military interventions and regime-change operations. In recent decades, such actions (in Vietnam, Cambodia, Laos, Guatemala, Haiti, Nicaragua, El Salvador, Afghanistan, Iran, Iraq, Libya, Yemen, and Syria, just to name a few) have led to repeated bloodbaths and disasters, not American victory and security.

Donald Trump's vision of America First is a racist and populist variant of traditional American exceptionalism. As a racist strategy, it will divide American society. As a populist strategy, it is doomed to fail and could create economic mayhem. As an exceptionalist foreign policy in a postexceptionalist era, it is likely to strengthen rather than weaken America's main competitors, especially China. Yet the most dangerous part of America First is that it could easily lead to war, even nuclear devastation. Foreign policy narcissism is extraordinarily perilous.

Since the late 1970s, the United States has been embroiled in wars and political upheavals in the Middle East. Before that, from the 1950s to 1970s, the United States was embroiled in Southeast Asia, and in the first half of the twentieth century in Latin America—different regions, same methods. As in those other regions, it would be both wise and timely for the United States to pack its bags and withdraw from Middle Eastern wars. These have been wars of choice, not wars of necessity, and they have been chronically poor choices.

The current nationalist wave makes even less sense than in the past, now that the entire world faces the challenges of severe environmental degradation and other global threats (such as newly emerging diseases and mass migration). These new challenges require global cooperation and international law, not nationalism and gauzy dreams of past glory (which are, alas, far more myth than reality). The world more than ever needs a United Nations configured for the twenty-first century and a commitment to shared objectives of sustainable development. At the core, U.S. foreign policy needs to shift from military might and warmaking to technological dynamism and global cooperation.

The logic of sustainable development should also draw us to the doctrine of *subsidiarity*. This important political and social doctrine holds that problems should be solved at the lowest feasible level of governance, the one closest to the people. Those problems that can be addressed by local governments (e.g., at the city level) should be. But not all can. Some require national solutions. Many, such as tapping renewable energy or controlling epidemic diseases, require strong regional cooperation at the scale of the European Union, or North America, or East Asia. Still others, such as controlling human-induced climate change and the massive loss of biodiversity around the world, require strong global cooperation and diplomacy.

I will take up these arguments in four sections. The first section discusses the history and limits of American exceptionalism, especially in an era when the rise of China and other parts of the world economy diminishes America's relative economic and military might. I discuss Trump's America First in the context of traditional American exceptionalism. The second section reconsiders America's addiction to regime change as a key, if not the key, instrument of foreign policy—especially in the Middle East, where the United States has been in nonstop war for a generation. I argue for the end of U.S. military engagement in the region. The third section takes up the economic merits of Trump's strategy and finds it likely to accelerate the relative decline of the United States. The fourth and final section offers my thoughts about how to restore U.S. diplomacy, especially to meet the challenges of sustainable development.

We stand poised between two possible futures—one of conflict, even nuclear war, and one of peaceful cooperation. To avoid the first and achieve the latter, we need a new American foreign policy, and a mind-set beyond exceptionalism. Our strength lies in our diversity and our ability to connect with all parts of the world in a cooperative spirit. These are the core messages I hope to convey in the coming chapters.

Part I

U.S. EXCEPTIONALISM IN A CHANGING WORLD

Americans tend to view the nation and its foreign policy in exceptional terms, with a history and a future unlike those of any other country. In recent decades, the United States has been seen as the "leader of the free world" and "the world's sole superpower." The result has been a kind of hubris, that the United States can dictate the terms of geopolitics and local politics to other parts of the world. Trump's America First doctrine is an especially crass version of this hubris, as it supposes that the United States can reject UN treaties and decisions, break trade agreements, maintain unrivaled military dominance in all parts of the world, and go it alone when it chooses.

As the old aphorism puts it, this is worse than a crime, it is a mistake. The United States lacks the economic and technological advantage to thumb its nose at the world. American economic power, in relative terms, has declined markedly in recent decades, most importantly because of the economic rise of Asia, especially China. The world is converging economically, meaning that gaps in income per capita and technological know-how are shrinking. No country in the world, neither the United States nor China, will dominate the rest in the twenty-first century.

As America's relative power has waned and others have begun to catch up, the United States has taken the increasing pushback as an affront. When the United States pushes NATO toward Russia's borders, and Russia reacts, the United States blames Russia for its belligerence, rather than also noting the provocations of its own policies. When the United States intervenes in Iraq, Syria, and Libya to overthrow regimes, and China and Russia rebuke the United States, the U.S. position has been to accuse those countries of being obstructionist.

What look like offensive actions by America's counterparts are often viewed as defensive actions by those same countries, a phenomenon known to political scientists as the "security dilemma." Defensive actions by one country look offensive to the other, thereby provoking escalation. Throughout this book, I'll invoke the security dilemma to encourage deeper scrutiny and understanding of world conflicts—from the world's point of view, as well as America's.

American exceptionalism could leave the United States on the sidelines as other parts of the world move forward. One notable case is the increasing economic and infrastructural integration of Eurasia, the giant land mass that is home to Europe and Asia. China has proposed the One Belt One Road initiative to link Asia and Europe in their common geographical home. The United States has so far stood aloof. Over time, Eurasia is likely to strengthen its economic, environmental, and investment cooperation. Instead of looking for dynamic new partnerships like these, the United States is falling back into old exceptionalist patterns—exemplified by revived tensions with Russia.

In this part, I will look at the history of American exceptionalism, its current manifestations, and what this vision misses.

1

FROM EXCEPTIONALISM
TO INTERNATIONALISM

American foreign policy today is uncertain and heatedly contested. The challenges of U.S. foreign policy are of fundamental significance for U.S. national security and well-being, and for global peace and prosperity. Americans must understand how the world has changed, and how we must change our attitudes and approaches along with it.

The new National Defense Strategy of the United States (which I'll consider in detail in chapter 9) takes a dark view of the world scene today: "We are facing increased global disorder, characterized by decline in the long-standing rules-based international order—creating a security environment more complex and volatile than any we have experienced in recent memory."[1] The world indeed seems to be a sea of problems: the ongoing Syrian war, the related European refugee crisis, ISIS and terrorist attacks across the globe, Russia's brazen hacking of the U.S. election, China's rising territorial claims in the South China Sea, North Korea's growing nuclear threat, and more.

Yet I will argue that this dark view is far too deterministic and pessimistic. The world also offers a host of new positive opportunities, if we understand them and build on them.

China, India, and the African Union are each home to more than a billion people with rapid economic growth and a rising middle class. The information revolution continues to advance at a dazzling rate. Robotics, artificial intelligence, and ubiquitous broadband offer the chances for dramatic breakthroughs in health care, education, and renewable energy, at home and globally.

If U.S. foreign policy is only about the threats and not the opportunities, the United States will miss out on the rapid advances in well-being that the new technological revolution can deliver, and that would help to stabilize today's conflict zones. The fundamental challenge facing U.S. foreign policy is to keep America safe without stumbling into needless wars, busting the military budget, breaking the world trade system, or diverting our attention and resources from the vital challenges of sustainable development.

The fiery debates around foreign policy, both today and throughout American history, are stoked by three competing visions of America's place in the world. These camps have fundamentally different views of what is possible and desirable in our interactions with other nations.

The first group, whom I call the "exceptionalists," argues that the United States should continue to aim for global dominance, maintained by unrivaled U.S. military superiority. This group sees U.S. military dominance as both feasible and necessary for global stability. One leading American exceptionalist, Ambassador Robert Blackwill, puts America's strategy this way: "Since its founding, the United States has consistently pursued a grand strategy focused on acquiring and maintaining preeminent power over various rivals, first on the North American continent, then in the Western hemisphere, and finally globally."[2] Blackwill and other exceptionalists argue that America's foreign policy, indeed its grand strategy, should be to preserve America's dominant power in the world. Trump's America First ideology is a variant of exceptionalism, adding xenophobia, racism, and protectionism to more traditional exceptionalist approaches.

The second group, whom I call the "realists," argues that the United States must accept a realistic balance of power rather than U.S. dominance. So far so good, in my view. Yet like the exceptionalists, the realists argue essentially for "peace through strength." They believe a new arms race is the necessary and inevitable price to pay to keep the balance of power and preserve U.S. security. I am adopting the term "realist" from its usage in political science. I don't mean that "realists" are necessarily more realistic, only that they adhere to the "Realist School" of international relations. As I will explain, I find realists to be unrealistic in crucial ways.

I am part of the third group, whom I call the "internationalists." Internationalists argue that global cooperation between nations is not only feasible but also essential to avoid war and to sustain American and global prosperity. In their view, global cooperation would spare the world a costly and dangerous new arms race between the United States and the emerging powers, one that could easily spill over into open conflict. Moreover, global cooperation would enable the United States and the world to seize the opportunities opened by today's technological revolution to boost economic growth while overcoming ills that include global warming, emerging diseases, and mass migration.

The term "internationalist" is sometimes used disparagingly. One might hear the gibe, "You're no patriot, you're an internationalist" as a typical gibe. The idea is that those who believe in global solutions are not really siding with the United States.

By embracing the term "internationalist," I want to underscore the basic idea that global cooperation boosts America's best interests along with those of the rest of the world. Internationalists believe strongly in win-win cooperation rather than in the win-lose competition emphasized by the exceptionalists and the realists.

The coming foreign policy battles will pit these three visions against each other, most likely in a fierce pitched battle for the hearts and minds of the American people. I am firmly in the internationalist camp. I believe that American exceptionalism is a dangerous illusion for America in the twenty-first century and that balance-of-power realism is excessively pessimistic about the potential for cooperative diplomacy.

Consider the current U.S. policy debate regarding China.

American exceptionalists see China's rise as an unacceptable threat to U.S. dominance. They argue that the United States should invest trillions of dollars in a new arms buildup in Asia, including ballistic missile defense for American allies. They argue that the benefits to the United States of a unilateral U.S. arms buildup would far exceed the costs, with benefits in the form of enhanced U.S. prestige, global leadership, national security, and the safety of overseas investments. They call for trade and technology measures to limit China's future economic growth. They call for a strengthened network of alliances.

Blackwill and Tellis put it this way:

> Because the American effort to 'integrate' China into the liberal international order has now generated new threats to U.S. primacy in Asia—and could eventually result in a consequential challenge to American power globally—Washington needs a new grand strategy toward China that centers on

balancing the rise of Chinese power rather than continuing to assist its ascendancy.[3]

To offer a simple numerical illustration: exceptionalists, I will suppose, call for a $5 trillion investment in new armaments, believing that this will enable the United States to extract $10 trillion in geopolitical advantages from China, for a net U.S. benefit of $5 trillion and loss to China of $10 trillion. For an American exceptionalist, the advantages of an arms buildup seem obvious, a no-brainer.

The realists agree with the exceptionalists that a unilateral U.S. military buildup will give the United States a net gain, but they believe that China will match the U.S. arms buildup. Even so, the realists argue that the United States should make the investment. Here is their reasoning.

If China invests $5 trillion in arms while the United States does not, then China will gain $10 trillion in geopolitical advantage. If both sides arm, each spending $5 trillion, neither side gains a geopolitical advantage or suffers a geopolitical loss. They arrive at a standoff, a balance of power. If the United States arms while China does not, the United States garners a net gain of $5 trillion, equal to $10 trillion in geopolitical benefits minus the $5 trillion cost of arms.

Using the jargon of game theory, the realists argue that an arms buildup is America's (and China's) "dominant" strategy. If China arms, then the United States should do so as well. If China does not arm, then the United States can secure a geopolitical advantage through its own military buildup. No matter what China does, therefore, the United States should arm. Since China reasons symmetrically, both countries end up arming, and each incurs a $5 trillion cost but ends up at a geopolitical standstill. According to the realists, the $5 trillion is the unavoidable cost to pay to ensure America's geopolitical parity with China.

Hold on, say the internationalists. Surely our two countries can come to their senses. The $5 trillion to be used for an arms race could be put toward more urgent needs, like education, health care, renewable energy, and infrastructure. Rather than an arms race, let's agree with China that neither side will arm. Better still, let's agree to pool some resources into new high-tech ventures to advance cutting-edge global solutions for low-carbon energy, quality education, health care for all, and other mutual goals, to achieve the kind of "smart, fair, and sustainable societies" that I wrote about in *Building the New American Economy*.

It is this kind of cooperation that the exceptionalists scoff at and that the realists believe to be unrealistic. Again, consider the words of Blackwill and Tellis:

> There is no real prospect of building fundamental trust, "peaceful coexistence," "mutual understanding," a strategic partnership, or a "new type of major country relations" between the United States and China. Rather, the most that can be hoped for is caution and restrained predictability by the two sides as intense U.S.-China strategic competition becomes the new normal, and even that will be no easy task to achieve in the period ahead.[4]

The essence of careful foreign policy analysis is to size up the contrasting positions.

The exceptionalists believe that, with enough investments, the United States can maintain its military dominance in Asia. The realists, for their part, feel that an arms race with China and with Russia is inevitable, no matter what the eventual outcome. They point to the bad behavior of China and Russia as evidence that diplomacy is very unlikely to succeed. China is busy expanding its military presence in the South China Sea. Russia is hacking U.S. politics, bombing Aleppo, and destabilizing Ukraine. How could the United States possibly trust those countries?

As an internationalist, I say, "Not so fast." China's and Russia's actions look aggressive from our point of view, but from the vantage points of China and Russia they are viewed as responses to U.S. actions. Recall the security dilemma—what looks like an offensive action to us may be a state's attempt to defend itself. Many Chinese strategists plausibly believe that the United States will try to stifle China's future economic growth and note that the United States outspends China on the military by more than two to one ($596 billion to $215 billion, in 2015), while deploying military bases in more than seventy countries, compared with China's sole foreign base in Djibouti. Considered through this lens, China hardly seems like the aggressor.

Russian strategists similarly argue that the United States, not Russia, provoked the deterioration of relations in recent years. They point to U.S. meddling in Russia's internal politics going back many years and, perhaps even more provocatively, to U.S. meddling in Ukraine as well. Russian strategists also strongly object to the U.S. attempts to make Ukraine a member of NATO—which would bring the U.S.-led military alliance right up to Russia's border—and to NATO's deployment of missile defense systems in Eastern Europe. Russia asserts that such missile defenses are designed to weaken Russian retaliation against U.S. aggression. (The new missile deployments follow America's unilateral withdrawal in 2002 from the U.S.-Soviet Anti-Ballistic Missile Treaty.)

President John F. Kennedy eloquently framed the debate between the realists and the internationalists (of which he was one) in a commencement speech at American University in 1963:

> Today the expenditure of billions of dollars every year on weapons acquired for the purpose of making sure we never need them is essential to the keeping of peace. But surely the acquisition of such idle stockpiles—which can only destroy and never create—is not the only, much less the most efficient, means of assuring peace. I speak of peace, therefore, as the necessary, rational end of rational men. I realize the pursuit of peace is not as dramatic as the pursuit of war, and frequently the words of the pursuers fall on deaf ears. But we have no more urgent task.[5]

Kennedy believed that the Cold War could be overcome, and the arms race halted and eventually reversed, through rational, mutually beneficial agreements.[6] In the same address, he offered this internationalist vision:

> So let us not be blind to our differences, but let us also direct attention to our common interests and the means by which those differences can be resolved. And if we cannot end now our differences, at least we can help make the world safe for diversity. For in the final analysis, our most basic common link is that we all inhabit this small planet. We all breathe the same air. We all cherish our children's futures. And we are all mortal.

This vision underpinned Kennedy's successful drive to negotiate the Partial Nuclear Test Ban Treaty in 1963, which in turn led to the Nuclear Non-Proliferation Treaty of 1968. Both treaties are an expression of the hopes and aspirations of internationalism: that a dangerous arms race can be slowed, and eventually reversed, through diplomacy and cooperation.

There is one more fundamental point to make about cooperation, demonstrated by game theory, tested in practice, and crucial for successful diplomacy. Cooperation is not blind trust, and it should not be naïve or unconditional. Internationalists like myself have no doubt that evil exists, and that Hitler bullied and duped the West with no intention other than war and conquest. When I speak about the gains from cooperation, it is on the basis of two beliefs: that the gains are large and mutual; and that if cooperation in fact breaks down, a country can still revert to the "realist" position.

In game theory, one such strategy of conditional cooperation is called Tit-for-Tat (TFT). The TFT strategy is to be cooperative at the start, but if the other side reneges, to revert to a tougher position and an arms race if necessary. Yet to sustain cooperation it's also very important not to be doctrinaire or to prejudge one's counterparts. Most importantly, it's vital not to mistake the defensive actions of those counterparts as aggression, or to assume that counterparts are incapable of cooperation. Both assumptions are likely to be dangerous and wrong, leading to a self-fulfilling arms race or worse.

Table 1.1 offers a schematic account of the three main foreign policy positions. As I summarize in the table, American exceptionalists believe in the dominance of American military power, the limits of cooperation, and the evil intentions of America's adversaries. Realists believe that U.S. military strength is needed because America's competitors will almost inevitably challenge American interests. Internationalists believe that humanity faces shared urgent challenges and

TABLE 1.1 Foreign Policy Positions

	Military power	Potential gains from cooperation	Likelihood of cooperation	Competition of values	Foreign policy
Exceptionalism	American dominance	Low	Low	American virtue in a world of evil	Military dominance, low priority on diplomacy
Realism	American advantage with strong adversaries	Moderate	Occasional	American values in a world of diverse values	Military buildup, cautious diplomacy
Internationalism	Rough parity of military power	High	High	Shared global values	Arms control, active diplomacy, shared global goals

vulnerabilities that make global cooperation necessary and achievable through rational diplomacy backed by threats if cooperation fails.

American exceptionalism, I will argue throughout this book, is passé, a throwback to the years after World War II when the United States dominated the world economy and was far ahead of the rest of the world in military and civilian technology. Times are very different now. The U.S. economy is actually smaller than China's when both are measured by a common set of international prices. It is still true today that U.S. military power is vast, with an unrivaled archipelago of military bases in dozens of countries. But we have seen repeatedly that U.S. firepower cannot enforce peace on the ground, much less the political outcomes sought by the United States.

Another fundamental change from the early postwar years is the much greater need for global cooperation regarding global warming, emerging diseases, and other environmental threats. If the United States and China come to view each other as military competitors, they are far less likely to view each other as partners in environmental sustainability. Our mind-set—conflict or cooperation—will shape not only our arms spending but also our chances to control global warming, fight newly emerging diseases, or invest together in new science and technology.

A third fundamental change is that the world now has the established institutional machinery to sustain global cooperation, thanks to more than seventy years of the United Nations and its various component institutions. It would be especially foolhardy and indeed reckless for the United States to turn its back on these global institutions—as indeed it is already starting to do, and as we'll consider further in chapter 15.

To make the world safe in the face of global warming and ensure the best life possible not just for Americans but for all the inhabitants of this small planet, we must reconsider long-held assumptions. American exceptionalism has reached a double dead end. It's no longer feasible, because the United States is no longer the dominant power that the exceptionalists imagine, and so it no longer works for guiding effective foreign policy—and hasn't for a while. Yes, the United States may have "won" the Cold War (in the exceptionalist telling), but it lost the Vietnam War and made a mess of wars and CIA adventurism in Southeast Asia, Africa, the Middle East, Central America, and other places where exceptionalism crashed against on-the-ground realities.

A continuation of American exceptionalism, whether in its traditional forms or in Trump's America First version, would spell further dangers and damage for the United States and for the world.

If we're smart, we can find a safe position for the United States without the claim of global dominance. Yet to do so we must reconsider a tenet that's been central to American identity for centuries—as we'll see in the next chapter.

2

EXCEPTIONALISM
AS THE CIVIC RELIGION

T he idea of American exceptionalism is deeply set in American culture and the institutions of foreign policy. We are addicted to an inflated self-image. How sadly appropriate, alas, to have a megalomaniac as president to proclaim America's continued dominance.

As many American historians have noted, American exceptionalism is deeply intertwined in America's history, or at least in one telling of it. When the first pilgrims arrived, they were not merely looking to establish a colony in the New World (which they regarded as "new" since they left the native Americans out of the accounting). They were establishing a "city upon the hill." America would be the new Promised Land.

This messianic vision provided the energy and vision to overcome the unimaginable difficulties of settling a new frontier thousands of miles from the European homelands. The European settlers faced famine and distance, resistance from indigenous populations, wars between the European powers, and of course growing tensions between the colonizers and the imperial governments back in Europe. At every turn, they called on Providence for their salvation, and at each victory, they gave credit to the Lord for supporting his new chosen people. America's success became divine success. America's strength became the proof of its divine mission in the world. In this, the Protestant settlers of New England followed the teachings of John Calvin: "There is no question that riches should be the portion of the godly rather than the wicked, for godliness hath the promise in this life as well as the life to come."[1]

The settlers, largely the descendants of the English and other peoples of the British Isles, arrived in the early seventeenth century at their Atlantic beachheads prepared to fight to stay, and then in God's name to spread across the American continent in the eighteenth and nineteenth centuries and the world in the twentieth century. In more than 250 years of almost continuous expansionist wars and bold investments in farms, factories, and infrastructure, Americans interpreted their successes as proof of the divinity of their cause.

In their exceptionalism, Americans were surely tutored by their English cousins, whose own global grandeur preceded America's global dominance by more than a century. For at least a century (roughly from 1815 to 1914), Britain seemed to be blessed with divine backing for true global dominance. Americans, many of them heirs to the same culture, language, and ethnicity, could look on with awe at the ever-expanding British Empire, no doubt with the secret hope, perhaps even expectation, that someday that empire would be their own.

American messianism revealed itself in the formative moments of the United States. It provided the fuel for the original settlements and for two centuries of war against native communities that stood in the ways of claims to the land and its natural wealth. It was carried in Lincoln's description of America as "the last best hope of Earth," even though it was the United States alone in the world that required a civil war to end slavery. It was epitomized by the idea of America's Manifest Destiny to occupy the lands between the oceans, notwithstanding the claims of other countries (such as Mexico) or the rights of the indigenous populations. It fueled the hubristic, yet wildly successful, Monroe Doctrine, by which a weak, start-up nation warned the great European powers to desist from meddling in the Americas.

Historians have noted that every major war of the United States has been cloaked in the language of America's divine mission to deliver not only success for itself but global salvation. At the end of the nineteenth century, just after the United States had fulfilled its "destiny" of ruling North America from ocean to ocean, the nation turned to overseas empire building. In 1898, it went to war against Spain, not to grab Spain's colonies but to liberate them (or so it claimed); 120 years later, the conquered lands—Cuba, Puerto Rico, and the Philippines—continue to bear the scars of U.S. intervention. Few residents of those countries would subscribe to the American view that they had been liberated by the United States.

In the twentieth century, the interventions abroad would be far larger and far more consequential for global history. On dozens of occasions, the United States sent its military into action in the Americas to overthrow governments, install pliant ones, grab territories (such as the Panama Canal Zone), secure investments in mines, oil, or farmlands, or suppress rebellions deemed to be hostile to American public or private interests. John Coatsworth has documented an astounding forty-one instances of U.S.-led "regime change" in the Americas, a pattern that would eventually be carried over to Africa, Europe, the Middle East, and Asia.[2] These are violent, extra-constitutional overthrows of foreign governments by the United States through a variety of means including wars, coups, assassinations, electoral manipulation, acts of provocation, and manufactured protests and mass unrest. Table 2.1 summarizes Coatsworth's remarkable findings, a careful undertaking that should be carried out systematically by specialists for all the world's regions, since America's regime-change operations have occurred not only in Latin America but also in dozens more cases in Asia, Europe, and Africa.

America's late entry into World War I was another messianic adventure with startling and unanticipated consequences for the world. When an unprecedented, industrial-scale bloodletting exploded in Europe in August 1914, the American public and its leaders generally urged the United States to stay clear of the European carnage. President Woodrow Wilson ran for reelection in 1916 on a platform to keep the United States out of war. Yet by 1917, Wilson decided that America's great economic and military power could be used not only to end the war but also to end all wars, a case of American grandiosity in action.

Before the U.S. intervention, the European combatants were locked in a grinding stalemate, one that might have ended in a truce without victor or vanquished. Yet America tilted the outcome to an outright victory by Britain and France over Germany and Austria. The idea of a peace without victors, an ostensible objective of the U.S. intervention, turned into the very opposite, a decisive defeat of the Hohenzollern (German) and Austro-Hungarian empires by France, Britain, and the United States that would subsequently result in a failed peace, economic chaos, the rise of Hitler, and a second world war one generation later. Americans tend to view the U.S. intervention in World War I as a success, but historians have explained with care the largely inadvertent damage caused by America's entry into the war.[3]

TABLE 2.1 Selected U.S. Interventions in Latin America, 1898–2004

Direct Interventions: Military/CIA activity that changed governments		
Cuba	1898–1902	Spanish-American War
	1906–1909	United States ousts elected president Tomás Estrada Palma; occupation regime
	1917–1923	U.S. reoccupation, gradual withdrawal
Dominican Republic	1916–1924	U.S. occupation
	1961	Assassination of President Trujillo
	1965	U.S. armed forces occupy Santo Domingo
Grenada	1983	U.S. armed forces occupy island, oust government
Guatemala	1954	C.I.A.-organized armed force ousts President Arbenz
Haiti	1915–1934	U.S. occupation
	1994	U.S. troops restore constitutional government
Mexico	1914	Veracruz occupied; United States allows rebels to buy arms
Nicaragua	1910	Troops to Corinto and Bluefields during revolt
	1912–1925	U.S. occupation
	1926–1933	U.S. occupation
	1981–1990	Contra war; then support for opposition in election
Panama	1903–1914	U.S. troops secure protectorate, canal
	1989	U.S. armed forces occupy nation

Indirect Interventions: Government/regime changes in which the United States was decisive		
Bolivia	1964	Military coup ousts elected president Paz Estenssoro
	1971	Military coup ousts General Torres
Brazil	1964	Military coup ousts elected president João Goulart
Chile	1973	Coup ousts elected president Salvador Allende
	1988–1989	Aid to anti-Pinochet opposition

(*continued*)

TABLE 2.1 *(continued)*

Cuba	1933	United States abandons support for President Machado
	1934	United States sponsors coup by Colonel Batista to oust President Grau
Dominican Republic	1914	United States secures ouster of General José Bordas
	1963	Coup ousts elected president Juan Bosch
El Salvador	1961	Coup ousts reformist civil-military junta
	1979	Coup ousts General Humberto Romero
	1980	United States creates and aids new Christian Democratic junta
Guatemala	1963	United States supports coup against elected president Miguel Ydígoras Fuentes
	1982	United States supports coup against General Lucas Garcia
	1983	United States supports coup against General Rios Montt
Guyana	1953	CIA aids strikes; government is ousted
Honduras	1963	Military coup ousts elected president Villeda Morales
Mexico	1913	U.S. Ambassador H. L. Wilson organizes coup against President Madero
Nicaragua	1909	Support for rebels against Zelaya government
	1979	United States pressures President Somoza to leave
Panama	1941	United States supports coup ousting elected president Arnulfo Arias
	1949	United States supports coup ousting constitutional government of President Chanís
	1969	United States supports coup by Genral Torrijos

Source: John H. Coatsworth, "Liberalism and Big Sticks: The Politics of U.S. Interventions in Latin America, 1898–2004" (Columbia University Academic Commons, 2006), https://academiccommons.columbia.edu /catalog/ac:204082https://academiccommons.columbia.edu/catalog/ac:204082.

The two world wars and a Great Depression between 1914 and 1945 crippled Europe, and by 1950, the North Atlantic leadership had passed to the United States. America's preeminence in war, peace, and the global economy was evident. U.S. industry became the arsenal of democracy, and Washington financed the war, but on terms that would ensure U.S. global economic dominance after the war. Alone among the great powers, America had come through the war unscathed on home territory (aside from the one-day attack on Pearl Harbor in December 1941).

In 1941, *Time* magazine editor Henry Luce proclaimed the American Century, the moniker under which the United States would exercise global leadership.[4] Americans quickly bought into the idea. It fit with a long-standing U.S. narrative: the United States as the exceptional country. And at the time, it was true. America's dominance by 1945 is hard to overstate. American industry had expanded to unprecedented dimensions, with the gross domestic product (GDP) in 1945 almost double that of 1939. As of 1950, the United States accounted for 27 percent of the world economy, compared with approximately 26 percent for Western Europe, 9 percent for the Soviet Union, and just 5 percent for China.

World War II had been the progenitor of breathtaking American innovations in science and technology, propelled by the demands of war: radar, sonar, ballistics, aeronautics, computers, semiconductors, cybernetics (human-machine interactions), applied mathematics, nuclear physics, chemistry, pharmaceuticals, metallurgy, and more. Europe's pre-Hitler scientific leadership arrived in the United States, refugee by refugee. The development of the atomic bomb was certainly the most visible symbol of the new cutting-edge physics harnessed to national power. But there were countless other crucial breakthroughs in science-based technology, as well as the realization that science-led development would be the key to economic advancement and to national security in the decades ahead.

By 1950, the United States had achieved unrivaled global leadership. It towered as perhaps the most powerful nation in world history. Although the Soviet Union, too, had nuclear arms after 1949, America's economic and technological preeminence in the civilian economy was unassailable. According to one estimate, by historian Angus Maddison, America's per capita GDP was 3.4 times that of the Soviet Union as of 1950.

The American Century was just getting started. How, then, could anyone doubt that Providence was on the side of the Americans, whose country had started as a tiny settlement hugging the Atlantic coast, spread across a continent, then across the oceans, and then across the world? (Of course that same delusion had gripped countless great powers before: Rome, Britain, Napoleon's France, China's Middle Kingdom, and many others).

It's worth reflecting on one important skeptical voice at midcentury, somebody who had thought a thing or two about God's purpose. Theologian Reinhold Niebuhr, at the moment of America's rise to global preeminence, had a foreboding that America's power would be its comeuppance, that America could be blinded by its might to its limitations, and even to right from wrong. Niebuhr warned Americans not to believe in their omniscience and omnipotence.[5] He warned about hubris, arrogance, and corruption by power and wealth as fundamental human traits and weaknesses. He worried that America's traditional messianism, its sense of carrying forward God's mission, and its easy equation of wealth with godliness would prove to be its undoing.

In short, Niebuhr presciently warned against the arrogance that came to be part and parcel of American overseas militarism after World War II. Niebuhr noted that the Calvinist credo that wealth is a sign of God's providence created an American culture "which makes 'living standards' the final norm of the good life" and "which regards the perfection of techniques [technology] as the guarantor of every cultural as well as of every social-moral value."[6] Niebuhr gave this wise warning, one that was not heeded by American leaders in future generations:

> Today the success of America in world politics depends on its ability to establish community with many nations, despite the hazards created by pride of power on the one hand and the envy of the weak on the other . . . [O]ur success in world politics necessitates a disavowal of the pretentious elements in our original dream, and a recognition of the values and virtues which enter into history in unpredictable ways.[7]

The United States assumed postwar leadership in several fundamental ways. Most creatively, and thanks to the political genius and vision of Franklin Roosevelt, the United States led the design and launch of the new United Nations bodies, including the Bretton Woods Institutions (World Bank and International Monetary Fund), the UN agencies (such as the World Health Organization), and other regional institutions. Beginning with Roosevelt's administration and continuing with Truman's, the United States also came to dominate global finance, providing large-scale development aid, official loans, and private capital investments for economic development. American companies, in the lead in new technologies, invested around the world. The dollar decisively replaced the pound sterling at the center of international finance and payments.

Yet internationalism was also matched by building a new security state. The United States invested heavily in the military and security agencies, eventually building a massive nuclear arsenal, hundreds of military bases around the world, several powerful intelligence agencies including the CIA, and military alliances to ensure continued U.S. dominance.

From 1945 to 1991, U.S. foreign policy was structured to prevail in the Cold War. Though the United States dominated the world economy, the communist bloc led by the Soviet Union formed a rival ideology and a geopolitical threat. "Containment" of the Soviet Union and of the spread of communism became the prevailing dogma, yet the concept was interpreted in three very different ways. U.S. exceptionalists viewed the Soviet Union as an incorrigible superpower intent on world domination, with the United States as the ultimate bulwark of global freedom. U.S. realists viewed containment in more traditional balance-of-power terms. Realists had no doubt that the Soviet Union would exploit Western political or military weaknesses where possible, but they did not believe that the Soviet Union was a juggernaut intent on taking over the world. U.S. internationalists, originally led by FDR himself, but then mainly on the U.S. political left, believed that the two blocs could not only coexist peacefully but also cooperate in areas of science, culture, and economic development. This view was rarely ascendant in U.S. foreign policy, except in brief periods such as 1963, when the United States and the Soviet Union concluded the Partial Nuclear Test Ban Treaty, and during periods of détente under Nixon, Ford, and Carter.

It is notable that the conceptual father of containment, George Kennan, bemoaned the exceptionalist interpretation, believing it to be dangerously hubristic, a naïve assertion of America's unique goodness and quest for global military dominance that was dangerous, unnecessary, and unachievable. In his 1957 BBC Reith Lectures, just a few years into the containment policy, Kennan put forward the proposition that a peace settlement regarding Germany, one that recognized Soviet security concerns, could actually remove the most important causes of the Cold War:

> I would know of no basic issues of genuine gravity between Russia and the West other than those arising directly from the manner in which the recent world war was allowed to come to an end. I am referring here particularly to the fact that the authority of a united German Government was expunged on the territory of Germany itself and throughout large areas of Eastern Europe, and the armies of the Soviet Union and the Western democracies were permitted to meet in the middle of this territory and to take control of it, before there was any adequate agreement among them as to its future permanent status.[8]

Kennan urged the West to consider one direction for a possible peaceful resolution: the unification of Germany outside of the North Atlantic Treaty Organization (NATO), thereby allowing for the mutual withdrawal from Germany of both NATO troops (in West Germany) and Soviet troops (in East Germany). Such compromise ideas found little support in the U.S. foreign policy community, and Kennan, though author of the original containment concept, found himself mostly outside of the mainstream after the mid-1950s.

The postwar U.S. security state had three faces. The public face included the United Nations linkages and the formal alliances like NATO, designed to keep the peace and to defend against Soviet aggression. The NATO alliance was established in 1949 mainly to defend against a possible Soviet invasion of Western Europe. The Federal Republic of Germany, or West Germany, which was formed in 1949 out of the zones of military occupation by the United States, Britain, and France, became a NATO member in 1955, largely closing the door on a settlement of World War II along the lines that Kennan envisaged. The first secretary-general of NATO, Lord Ismay, famously declared that the purpose of NATO was "to keep the Soviet Union out, the Americans in, and the Germans down." This meant that NATO would commit the United States to the defense of Western Europe, would prevent a Soviet invasion, and would subordinate German military and industrial might to a larger, U.S.-led alliance.

The public face of the security state largely maintained an internationalist perspective, aligning the United States with the United Nations and its new institutions to help promote cooperation when that could be established. Thus, the United States was leader of the "free world" (backed by the NATO alliance) as well as the leader of global cooperation through the UN institutions and agencies. Yet when the United States faced limits within the UN—for example, when opposed by the Soviet Union and its allies—the United States was hardly shy about asserting national prerogatives despite UN opposition.

A second, more shrouded face, was in the contested postcolonial world. Would the newly independent countries swing toward the United States or the Soviet Union? Open warfare, secret CIA operations including regime changes and assassinations of foreign leaders, and bribes and other inducements were used to keep countries in the U.S. camp. The CIA, created in 1947, became a secret army of the U.S. president,

carrying out coups, assassinations, and destabilization operations against governments deemed hostile to U.S. security
interests. Alas, the CIA not only poisoned local politics in
places where it intervened but also poisoned the rule of law in
the United States, with presidents becoming knowing accomplices to murder and mayhem.

The third face was the most cynical of the three. Even when
Soviet influence was nowhere to be seen, American interests
might be at stake, as when a reform-minded government in
Guatemala in the early 1950s decided on land reform to benefit the landless peasants. That was quite enough of a threat
for the American company United Fruit International, which
called its U.S. law firm Sullivan and Cromwell in 1954 to mobilize its former associates John Foster Dulles (U.S. secretary of
state) and Allen Dulles (director of the CIA). Soon enough,
Guatemala's reform-minded leader, Jacobo Arbenz, was overthrown. And Guatemala was hardly alone. With God on its
side, the United States would overthrow dozens of leaders over
the coming decades, many by outright assassination, and many
in the pursuit of oil, farmlands, and other commercial benefits
rather than anything resembling true national security.

What has been the legacy of these three facets of the U.S.
security state? The balance sheet is mixed at best, often quite
grim, and in recent years decidedly negative.

The most positive part of the new security arrangements,
harnessing the United States to the United Nations, lasted
for perhaps twenty years. Presidents Truman, Eisenhower,
and Kennedy gave considerable focus and support to the
United Nations and backed its nascent institutions. Of
course, all three also unleashed countless acts of aggression
and covert operations wholly contrary to the UN Charter.
Yet by the time of President Nixon, even the priority given

to UN decision making began to wane. Presidents generally sought UN approval when they could get it and acted without it when they could not, with variations on this theme across U.S. administrations. The internationalists, who had been led by Franklin Roosevelt's vision of the UN, gradually lost their hold on U.S. foreign policy. They believed that the Cold War could be largely avoided by recognizing the Soviet Union's valid security needs (such as a peace agreement with Germany), yet this more cooperative view was never really put to the test.

America's core military alliances, with NATO, Japan, Korea, and others, mostly kept the peace, but with the near-miracle of dodging several close brushes with nuclear war caused by blunders, saber-rattling, misunderstandings, bluffs, and false alarms. The world was saved, on several occasions, by sheer dumb luck and by a few people who had more sense than the "sophisticated" security systems in which they were embedded.

NATO's role after the 1991 dissolution of the Soviet Union has been far more problematic. Despite the end of NATO's core mission—to protect Western Europe from a Soviet invasion—NATO not only stayed in existence but also expanded to the east toward Russia, sounding alarm bells in Russia and stoking a new Cold War. NATO forces bombed a European capital (Belgrade) in 1999 and flew combat missions in Libya in 2011 to topple Moammar Khadafy, giving rise to the accusations of dangerous NATO "mission creep" in the service of American military dominance.

The proxy wars worked out far worse. The United States has been in almost nonstop war since 1945. When facing the Soviet Union, every local fluctuation of power, every war of national liberation, every civil war, was viewed by the U.S.

security state through the Cold War lens. Would a victory by side A or side B be better for the United States or the Soviet Union? Suddenly, the United States decided it had vital stakes in every local conflict, whether in Vietnam, Cambodia, and Laos in the 1950s–1970s, Central America in the 1980s, Africa in the 1980s and 1990s, the Balkans in the 1990s, or the Middle East almost continuously from the 1970s onward. America notoriously overestimated the unity of "global communism," as if every self-proclaimed Marxist state or revolutionary faction in the world was taking direct orders from Moscow.

There is one overriding lesson from all these proxy wars: No superpower wins, but the locals inevitably lose, and lose badly. Millions have died at U.S. hands, with very little recognition by Americans of the carnage they are creating. Most recently, America's hand in the Syrian war, led secretly by the CIA in partnership with Saudi Arabia, has been disastrous for Syria. Ten million Syrians have been displaced and hundreds of thousands have died, with no benefit for Syria's long-term governance. Yet, despite America's devastating role in Syria, most Americans would likely answer that the United States hasn't even been at war in Syria, since their newspapers did not cover the covert CIA-Saudi activities.

The third face—the secretive, self-serving actions by the United States to defend U.S. commercial interests—has had a very bad yet predictable habit of returning to bite us. Americans have repeatedly overthrown governments for American financial convenience only to be thrown out later by a subsequent turn of politics. America's repeated backing for dictatorships who defend U.S. business interests ends up being what is called an "obsolescing bargain," one that may start well (for narrow U.S. commercial interests) but end badly for the United States in the longer term.

Think of America's cynical overthrow of Iran's prime minister Mohammad Mosaddeq in 1953, in order to defend British and U.S. claims to Iran's oil. The U.S. installed the Shah of Iran, who ruled with his secret police until 1979. After that, the United States predictably and understandably became the Great Satan for the Iranian Revolution that followed. Or think of America's backing of the corrupt despot Batista in Cuba, followed by the Cuban Revolution. The list of such blowbacks is long indeed, as I'll explore in further detail in chapter 6.

American exceptionalism turned especially destructive after the end of the Cold War. Since 1992, the United States has fought several devastating wars—in Afghanistan, Iraq, Syria, Libya, Yemen, Somalia, and elsewhere—without achieving the political outcomes it sought. The link between these wars and the end of the Cold War is not incidental. Former NATO commander Wesley Clark spelled out the linkage in several books and interviews. After the first Gulf War in 1991, General Clark dropped into the Pentagon to see Paul Wolfowitz, the undersecretary of defense for policy at the time. Wolfowitz told Clark that "we did learn one thing that's very important" from the Gulf War:

> With the end of the Cold War, we can now use our military with impunity. The Soviets won't come in to block us. And we've got five, maybe 10, years to clean up these old Soviet surrogate regimes like Iraq and Syria before the next superpower emerges to challenge us . . . We could have a little more time, but no one really knows.[9]

Here was the exceptionalist agenda in the hands of a new generation of hard-liners (Wolfowitz, his boss Donald Rumsfeld, Richard Cheney, and others). America would "clean up" the Middle East through violent regime change. In truth, it was the old playbook, yet in an especially treacherous part of the world. And the consequences have demonstrated the sheer hubris and incompetence of the effort.

The Middle East wars not only failed politically but they also cost trillions of dollars, financed largely by deficit spending and rising public debt. The ratio of U.S. public debt to GDP soared from 34 percent in 2000 to around 76 percent in 2016. In the meantime, America's reputation in the world plummeted, and the United States ceased to be viewed as a constructive partner for global problem solving. And in the midst of the Middle East wars, Wall Street visited a virulent financial crisis on the world, itself produced in no small part through hubris and financial criminality, again with almost no accountability for the miscreants.

For a country steeped in the mythos of global salvation, we have run dangerously off course. American exceptionalism has guided us into endless war and driven us deeply into debt. Yet just when it's most crucial that we step back to the internationalist position championed by Roosevelt with the creation of the United Nations, we are moving in exactly the opposite direction.

EXCEPTIONALISM IN THE ERA OF TRUMP

Donald Trump's "America First" foreign policy represents a new and vulgar strain of American exceptionalism. It proudly proclaims its intention to maintain U.S. military dominance as the core pillar of U.S. foreign policy. Trump's National Security Strategy (NSS) uses the term "overmatch" to signify this military dominance:

The United States must retain overmatch—the combination of capabilities in sufficient scale to prevent enemy success and to ensure that America's sons and daughters will never be in a fair fight. Overmatch strengthens our diplomacy and permits us to shape the international environment to protect our interests. To retain military overmatch the United States must restore our ability to produce innovative capabilities, restore the readiness of our forces for major war, and grow the size of the force so that it is capable of operating at sufficient scale and for ample duration to win across a range of scenarios.[10]

A fundamental pillar of Trump's America First exceptionalism is therefore the intention to invest massively in a new arms race with China, Russia, and other adversaries.

America First introduces several distinctive strains, however. The first is a naked nationalism in a world of clashing interests. "We are prioritizing the interests of our citizens and protecting our sovereign rights as a nation," writes Trump in his cover letter to the new strategy. "A central continuity in history is the contest for power. The present time is no different," states the NSS. "China and Russia want to shape a world antithetical to U.S. values and interests"—antithetical to, not merely competitive with.

The second is racism. America First is really White America First. Trump's electoral campaign against "Mexican rapists" and "Muslim terrorists," his failures to denounce American white supremacists, his attack on immigration to the United States from "shithole" countries including Haiti and African nations, his call for more immigration from countries like Norway, all play directly to his electoral base: older, less-educated, white Americans.

In this regard, Trump is part of a worldwide wave of anti-immigrant and racist politics stoked by the large-scale migration and refugee movements of the past quarter century. Trump also represents the latest virulent outbreak of America's long history of racism. As I recount in chapter 17, America's 1924 Immigration Act was indeed designed to spur immigration from the Nordic countries. Not surprisingly, it was much appreciated by Hitler and the Nazi immigration lawyers.

The third distinctive strain of America First exceptionalism is economic populism, albeit of a Trumpian variety. Populism, in name, means an appeal to the average person, the "common man and woman," against special interests. I have no problem, and indeed I have much sympathy, with this sentiment. Where populists like Trump go wrong is that they stir their followers with simplistic diagnoses and promises that they cannot fulfill. Then, to try to rescue themselves, they usually raid the treasury, with deficit spending to eke out more time in power. They typically fall from power when their promises of higher living standards fail to materialize, and the budget deficits produce high inflation or a solvency crisis.

Trump's economic populism has some important distinctive elements. First, unlike typical populism, Trump's policies are benefiting mainly the rich rather than his working-class base of voters. A truly populist tax cut would have given most of the benefits to workers and their families, not to wealthy and powerful corporations, as is in fact the case. As is often the case with economic populists, Trump's tax cut will increase the budget deficit, putting added strains on future budgetary policies and inflation.

Second, Trump's economic populism takes aim at foreigners, further shielding America's own rich from scrutiny and fiscal accountability. Trump has told his working-class followers that their travails are due mainly to illegal migrants and overseas Mexican and Chinese workers, all of whom, Trump claims, have taken the jobs of hardworking (mainly white) Americans. They've gotten away with it, according to Trump, because American trade negotiators have given away the store to Mexico, China, and other foreign countries.

As I explained in *Building the New American Economy*, Trump's view is nonsense.[11] Yes, trade has opened the gap between rich and poor in the U.S. economy, not because of unfair trade practices abroad or bad trade negotiations but because the United States exports capital-intensive goods in return for labor-intensive imports from abroad. The expansion of this kind of trade indeed widens inequality in the United States, but the correct response is to keep trade open (which enlarges the overall U.S. and world economy) while redistributing income from America's rich to the poor, a solution that runs diametrically opposite to Trump's policies of aiding the rich at the expense of the poor.

All of this raises an ultimate question. For whose benefit is America First? Is the arms buildup really designed to promote U.S. national security? Is the sale of hundreds of billions of dollars of armaments to Middle Eastern nations really designed to promote peace? Was the 2017 tax cutting really designed to boost living standards of average households? Is the emerging economic war with China really to raise the well-being of typical Americans?

Perhaps the one overriding truth of America politics in recent decades is the overarching political power of the main corporate lobbies: the military-industrial complex, Wall Street, Big Oil, and Big Health Care.[12] Perhaps the best way to understand Trump's economic policies is to focus not on his populist rhetoric but on the interests of the powerful corporate lobbies. The tax cuts and anti-environmental actions of the Trump administration certainly favor Big Oil, Wall Street, the military-industrial complex, and Big Health Care. In the name of populism, we see a policy of corporatism—putting the companies, not America, first. As with most populisms, Trump's variety is almost sure to breed significant disappointment among Americans, including Trump's own political base.

American exceptionalism today is more than ever divorced from reality. This is a hard truth, and one that many Americans are not yet willing to accept—as evidenced by the unexpected electoral success of Trump's rallying cry to "make America great again." For Trump and the exceptionalists like him, the United States is still the unrivaled and unmatched global superpower. America's economy is still number 1, as long as the unfairness of foreigners is checked and brought under control. In truth, the remedies for America's security and economic needs lie not in bashing foreigners, expanding the arms race, cutting corporate taxes, or increasing the budget deficit. The real answers lie in global cooperation; a boost of critical investments at home in education, skills, technology, and environmental protection; and more help for the poor, paid for by more tax collections, rather than yet another round of tax cuts, and by savings from a bloated military budget.

3

THE ERA OF GLOBAL CONVERGENCE

I n book four of *The Wealth of Nations*, published in 1776, Adam Smith described the early events of globalization that commenced with Christopher Columbus's discovery of the sea route from Europe to the Americas in 1492 and Vasco da Gama's voyage from Europe to India in 1498. "The discovery of America, and that of a passage to the East Indies by the Cape of Good Hope, are the two greatest and most important events recorded in the history of mankind,"[1] wrote Smith. History has vindicated Smith's judgment. It is our generation's fate to usher in another fundamental chapter of globalization, one that requires a rethinking of foreign policy by the United States and other world powers.

Smith noted that globalization should raise global well-being, "by uniting, in some measure, the most distant parts of the world, by enabling them to relieve one another's wants, to increase one another's enjoyments, and to encourage one another's industry." Smith believed that international commerce and the "mutual communication of knowledge" (the international flow of ideas and technology) would hasten that day of equality.

Smith did recognize that, in the first wave of globalization following the voyages of Columbus and da Gama, the native populations of the Americas and Asia suffered because Europe's "superiority of force" enabled the Europeans to "commit with impunity every sort of injustice," including enslavement and political domination. Yet Smith also foresaw a future era in which the native populations "may grow stronger, or those of Europe grow weaker" to arrive at an "equality of courage and force" that could lead to a mutual "respect for the rights of one another."

In short, Adam Smith foresaw a world in which global trade and the flow of ideas would enrich all parts of the world, not just the European powers that initiated globalization, or the North Atlantic (Western Europe, the United States, and Canada) that first industrialized and dominated the world economy and geopolitics during the nineteenth and twentieth centuries.

Smith's vision has arrived. Our generation is at a cusp of history, in which centuries of European (and later American) global ascendancy are now being counterbalanced by the rise of "native populations" in Asia, Africa, the Middle East, and the Americas. U.S. foreign policy during the past seventy-five years, and arguably during the past 125 years, has been premised on a world economy led by the North Atlantic region, meaning Western Europe and the United States. That kind of North Atlantic globalization is now reaching an end. The tensions we see now around the world are symptomatic of the passing of the old order.

It is useful to chart the changing shares of the world's population and output from 1500 until 2008, as estimated by historian Angus Maddison. This is done in figure 3.1 for population, and figure 3.2 for output, for two major groups: the West and Asia. The West is defined here as Western Europe plus four "Western offshoots" (Maddison's phrase): the United States,

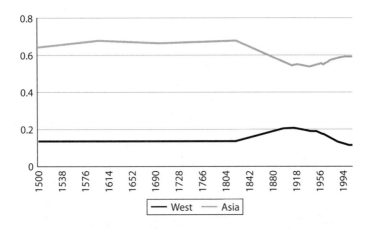

FIGURE 3.1 The West and Asia: Shares of world population. Data from Maddison Project Database, version 2010, https://www.rug.nl/ggdc/historicaldevelopment/maddison/releases/maddison-database-2010.

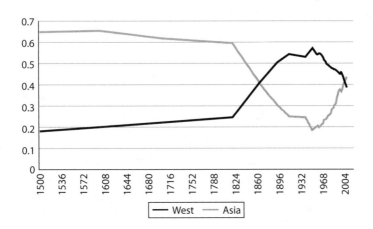

FIGURE 3.2 The West and Asia: Shares of world output. Data from Maddison Project Database, version 2010, https://www.rug.nl/ggdc/historicaldevelopment/maddison/releases/maddison-database-2010.

Canada, Australia, and New Zealand. Asia includes East Asia, South Asia, Western Asia, and Central Asia.

The main point is this. In 1500, Asia was home to roughly two-thirds of the world's population and two-thirds of the world's output. The world was overwhelmingly poor and rural, and the world's populous agrarian empires were in East and South Asia. By 1913, following a century of Western industrialization, the world economy was now mostly in the West, which hosted a remarkable 54 percent of global output with only 20 percent of the world's population. Asia's share of the world economy had declined precipitously, to only 25 percent of global output despite having 55 percent of the world's population.

While the age of discovery and commerce after Columbus gave Europe footholds in Asia and led to European conquests of the Americas, it was the Industrial Revolution that began in England around 1750—ushered in by the steam engine, large-scale steel production, scientific farming, and the mechanization of textiles—that truly created the Western-led global economy. By 1900, the world economy was largely in Europe's hands, both economically and politically. Asia was still the center of the global population, but no longer of the world economy.

Note specifically what had happened to China. According to the estimates, China's share of the world economy was as high as 33 percent in 1820 but only 9 percent by 1913. By 1950, after four decades of revolution, civil war, and invasion by Japan, China's share of world output had sunk to just 5 percent, probably the lowest in 2,000 years.

Britain was the first industrial nation, and the British Empire (including the United Kingdom, Canada, Australia, India, and other imperial possessions) dominated the world

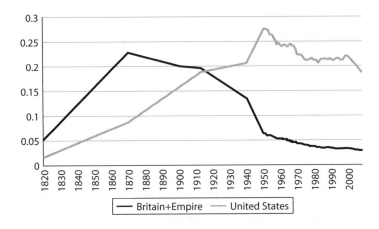

FIGURE 3.3 Shares of world output: Britain + Empire and United States. Data from Maddison Project Database, version 2010, https://www.rug.nl/ggdc/historicaldevelopment/maddison/releases/maddison-database-2010.

economy during the nineteenth century. The economic rise of Britain plus its empire is charted in figure 3.3. There I show the share of world output accounted for by Britain and its empire, alongside the share of the United States. The British Empire constituted the largest economic bloc in the world until the eve of World War I, when the United States equaled the empire in overall size. From the next century, the United States became the largest economy in the world, until it was overtaken by China in 2014 (according to IMF estimates).

During the second half of the nineteenth century, and at least until the start of World War I, the City of London dominated global finance and the British Navy ruled the seas. The era of British dominance is sometimes called *Pax Britannica*, but *pax* (peace) was a rosy description of an era when Europe was fighting and conquering lands throughout Africa and Asia, and suppressing violent insurrections (known as "terrorism" to the Europeans) that grew from local resistance to European rule. Britain in particular applied the foreign policy of regime change as the basis of long-term imperial rule. If a particular government in a poor, remote country threatened British interests, toppling the regime and replacing it with a friendly regime was always an option. (Twentieth-century America learned well from the British method of statecraft.)

Britain's precipitous decline began with World War I, which stripped Britain of financial wealth and left the young generation dead on Europe's killing fields. The interwar period, 1918–1939, was marked by a decade of instability (1918–1929) followed by the decade of worldwide Great Depression (1929–1939). World War II again utterly devastated Britain, physically, financially, and psychologically. By 1945, the baton of global leadership had decisively passed from Britain to the United States, which was eager to play its new role.

In a key insight, the late economic historian Charles Kindleberger observed that the 1930s was an interregnum between British global economic leadership to the 1920s and American leadership from the early 1940s onward.[2] In Kindleberger's interpretation, the Great Depression occurred with such ferocity, depth, and persistence because there was no single leader to stop the crisis. Britain was too weak to contain the depression, while the United States was too inexperienced to take the global mantle of leadership. Indeed, the United States insisted on facing the Great Depression on strictly national terms, without an orchestrated global recovery effort.

Months after the start of World War II, with France's quick capitulation to Nazi Germany and Britain's near defeat soon after, the United States and the Soviet Union became the last redoubts against German domination of Europe. Churchill famously declared that Britain would fight on, from Canada if necessary, until the New World came to the rescue of the Old. The United States did step in, but it lent—rather than gave—Britain the armaments to fight Hitler. As a result, Britain was in debt to the United States, and the United States was well positioned to replace Britain as the dominant world power.

The end of World War II marked (by and large) the end of the European empires in Africa and Asia, though the process of decolonization stretched out over decades and was often violent. The United States often confused decolonization with the Cold War and therefore became a voluntary heir to various anticolonial struggles (which I'll look at in more detail in chapter 6)—most notably and destructively in Vietnam, where the United States fought unsuccessfully against the national unity of Vietnam for two decades after France's withdrawal in 1955. Similarly, the United States tried to assert its will in the postcolonial Middle East, in part to keep the Soviet Union out and in part to keep America's oil companies in.

With Europe's empires gone, the newly independent nations of Africa and Asia had a new opportunity to invest in their own futures, especially in education, public health, and infrastructure. At least some of the countries made good on that opportunity. China began to stir with the establishment of the People's Republic of China in 1949. What had been 200 years of growing European dominance began to give way to a process of "catching up," whereby at least some of the formerly colonized countries began to adopt modern technologies, spread literacy and disease control, and generally achieve economic development at a pace faster than in the leading North Atlantic countries through incorporation into global production systems. The gap between the North Atlantic leaders and developing-country "followers" finally began to narrow.

The greatest success story was Asia. First, Japan quickly recovered from World War II and began to build an industrial powerhouse. Then came the "Asian tigers": Hong Kong, Singapore, Taiwan, and South Korea. And then came China, with the market reforms commencing in 1978, when Deng Xiaoping ascended to power after Mao Zedong's death. Asia's example inspired market reforms in Eastern Europe and the Soviet Union from the mid-1980s, made possible by the rise to power of Mikhail Gorbachev. The initial results were more political than economic. Eastern Europe peacefully broke away from the Soviet Union in 1989, and then the Soviet Union itself dissolved into its fifteen republics at the end of 1991.

In 1992, U.S. exceptionalists looked out over the world and saw confirmation of their vision of a U.S.-led (and dominated) world. The great enemy was gone. The bipolar power structure of the United States and the Soviet Union was now a unipolar world, and the "End of History"—as Francis Fukuyama famously termed the era, seeing it as "the end point of mankind's ideological evolution and the universalization of Western liberal democracy as the final form of human government"[3]—was, they imagined, at hand.

What the exceptionalists didn't realize is that 1992 would also mark an inflection point in the acceleration of China's growth. Figure 3.4 shows the U.S. and Chinese share of world output from 1820 until today, using estimates by Angus Maddison for 1820–1979 and the International Monetary Fund for 1980–2017. America's share of world output peaked in 1950 and has been on a gradual decline since then. China's output share was very low during most of the century (less than 5 percent, compared with a share of global population of around 20 percent) but then soared after 1978. In 1992,

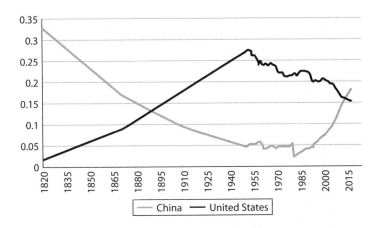

FIGURE 3.4 Shares of world output: China and United States. Data from Maddison Project Database, version 2010, https://www.rug .nl/ggdc/historicaldevelopment/maddison/releases/maddison -database-2010.

the United States produced 20 percent of world output and China a mere 5 percent. After a quarter-century of super-charged Chinese growth, in 2016 the U.S. share had declined to 16 percent and China's had slightly overtaken the United States at 18 percent (according to IMF estimates). China has caught up with history.

Moreover, the surge of information technology, which will underpin the next generation of global economic growth, is spreading rapidly throughout the world; the technological revolution will create global wealth, not U.S. wealth alone. China is now by the far the world's largest Internet user, with around 740 million users in mid-2017, compared with around 290 million American users.[4] Broadband access is soaring in all regions of the world, and Internet-based information and communications technologies (ICTs) will transform virtu-ally every sector of the modern world economy: agriculture, mining, manufacturing, energy, transportation, finance, law, medicine, public administration, and others. The United States will not be the only, and often not the first, country to make the transformation to the new ICT-based systems. These will be developed and deployed in all parts of the world.

Population trends will also shift the weight of the world economy toward Asia and Africa. Consider this: In 1950, the United States, Canada, and Europe constituted 29 percent of the world's population. By 2015, this had declined to 15 percent. By 2050, the share will decline further, perhaps to around 12 percent (based on UN projections[5]). Africa, by contrast, had just 9 percent of the world's population in 1950, 15 percent in 2015, and around 25 percent expected as of 2050. The U.S. share of the world population in 2050 will be around 4 percent, not too far from its current share.

Here is the key point: The dominance of the North Atlantic was a phase of world history that is now closing. It began with Columbus, took off with James Watt and his steam engine, was institutionalized in the British Empire until 1945 and then in the so-called American century, but has now run its course. The United States remains strong and rich, but no longer dominant.

We are not heading into the China century, or the India century, or any other, but a world century. The rapid spread of technology and the near-universal sovereignty of nation-states means that no single country or region will dominate the world in economy, technology, or population. This is especially true because China's share of the world's population will decline sharply, and with it, China's share of world output. As of 2015, China constituted 20 percent of world population and roughly 18 percent of world output. According to the UN "medium-fertility" projection shown in figure 3.5, China's

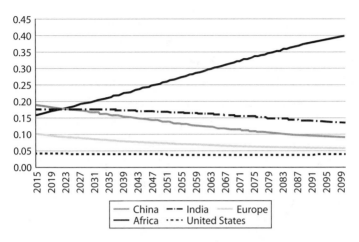

FIGURE 3.5 Population shares by major countries and regions, 2015–2100: UN medium-fertility projection

Source: United Nations, Department of Economic and Social Affairs, Population Division, *World Population Prospects: The 2017 Revision*, Volume I: Comprehensive Tables, https://esa .un.org/unpd/wpp/publications/Files/WPP2017_Volume-I_Comprehensive-Tables.pdf.

share of the world's population will decline to 10 percent by 2100. It will be Africa's rapidly growing population that will soar as a share of the world's total.

Moreover, with world population growth slowing and the world population aging, countries will be populated by older people. The median age of the Chinese population (the age at which half are older and half younger) was twenty-four years in 1950 and rose to thirty-seven years as of 2015. It is projected to rise to fifty years by 2050. Americans, too, will be no spring chickens, with a median age of forty-two years as of midcentury. History has shown that a bulge of youth in the population has often been tinder for conflict; now we will have a bulge of the elderly.

The United States must rethink its foreign policy exceptionalism in a world that has changed fundamentally, with rapid "catch-up" growth in Asia and now Africa, a worldwide IT revolution still picking up speed, and major changes in global population patterns. The great foreign policy challenge of our age will be to manage cooperation among many competing and technologically advanced regions, and most urgently to face up to our common environmental and health crises. We should move past the age of empires, decolonization, and cold wars. The world is arriving at the "equality of courage and force" long ago foreseen by Adam Smith—but unless we adopt a new foreign policy, we will find that the world has left us behind as we stubbornly insist on going it alone.

4

EURASIA ON THE RISE, AMERICA ON THE SIDELINES

A s an indication of America's waning "exceptionalism," the world's biggest geopolitical trend today has nothing to do with the United States. It is the economic integration of Europe with Asia, especially the European Union with China. Europe and Asia co-inhabit the world's largest landmass, Eurasia. They are increasingly connected economically as well. Trump's protectionism and bellicosity will only speed up the integration of Europe and Asia, leaving the United States on the sidelines.

Geologists tell us that as a landmass Eurasia has existed for around 70 million years. And demographers tell us that Eurasia has been home to roughly two-thirds of humanity during at least the past two thousand years. Trade, migration, wars, and ideas have linked Europe and Asia throughout history (and prehistory). As Jared Diamond pointed out in his wonderful book *Guns, Germs, and Steel,*[1] the diffusion of technologies between Asia and Europe has been facilitated by Eurasia's broad east-west orientation along climate zones. For example, wheat is grown in similar climate zones in Western Europe, Eastern Europe, Western Asia (e.g., Turkey, Iraq, and Iran), the northern stretches of South Asia (e.g., Pakistan and

India), and East Asia (e.g., Myanmar and China), a wheat belt stretching some ten thousand kilometers. This Eurasian wheat belt, by dint of sharing a core underlying technology and ecology, has been a vast corridor of cultural, technological, artistic, and economic exchange and interaction for thousands of years.

Throughout history, technological breakthroughs in one part of Eurasia have gradually diffused to others. Between AD 500 and AD 1500, technological dynamism was mostly in Asia (e.g., China), and technologies flowed from China to Europe. After 1800, the technological dynamism was mostly in Western Europe, with technological innovations flowing from Europe to Asia. Now both Europe and Asia are innovators, and new technologies are flowing in both directions.

From the 1500s to the 1700s, economic interactions between East Asia and Europe were scant; both China and Japan limited contacts with Europeans as a matter of national security. With the beginnings of European industrialization, interactions intensified, but not so happily for Asia. Britain and France conquered large swaths of Asia and held China at gunpoint to open its borders to trade, including the import of opium, forced on China by British opium traders and the British government. As the costs of transport and communications continued to decline with improvements in technology, European-Asian trade intensified, but with the military power and market advantage on the side of the Europeans.

The prospects for Asian development improved with India's independence in 1947 and the birth of the People's Republic of China in 1949. Both countries embarked on campaigns of mass literacy as a foundation for industrialization. Then China opened to international trade in 1978 and India in 1991, giving those population giants a massive positive jolt to economic growth. China's GDP grew at around 9.7 percent per year between 1980 and 2016, for a cumulative growth in national income of around twenty-eight times. India's economy grew fast but less dynamically, at around 6.3 percent per annum, with cumulative GDP growth of around nine times. Recently, India's economic growth of around 7.6 percent per year has been slightly higher than China's.

From 1950 to 2000, the United States was the world's leading economy and the main builder of global production networks. American multinational companies expanded their operations in both Europe and Asia (especially East Asia), with the United States the hub of new technology, global finance, and military security.

During the heyday of U.S. economic dominance, Europe's exports were directed mainly toward the U.S. market. In 1980, for example, Europe's $44 billion in exports to the United States were much larger than its $33 billion in exports to East, South, Southeast, and Central Asia. Yet with the dramatic rise of the Asian economies after 1980, Europe's exports are increasingly heading toward Asia. By 2015, Europe's $446 billion in exports to the United States were less than its $659 billion in exports to East, South, Southeast, and Central Asia.

The costs of trade between Europe and Asia are falling rapidly with continuing advances in information and communications technologies and related improvements in air, sea, and land transport and logistics. And as China's economy has soared, China's increasingly competitive multinational companies are stepping up their search for other markets, first in Southeast and Central Asia, but also in the Middle East, South Asia, Russia, resource-rich Africa, and Western Europe. China is now actively building long-distance transport, communications, and energy infrastructure links with other parts of Asia and between Asia and Europe, in the same way that the United States once supported Europe's and Japan's infrastructure development after World War II in order to foster export markets and production sites for American companies.

As China builds its trade and infrastructure links within Asia and with Europe, it harks back to Eurasia's history for inspiration. Chinese leaders describe the infrastructure efforts as building the new Silk Road, referring to the ancient trade routes that connected China by land with Central Asia, South Asia, the Middle East, and Europe for almost 2,000 years, until the 1600s:

> For thousands of years, the Silk Road Spirit—"peace and cooperation, openness and inclusiveness, mutual learning and mutual benefit"—has been passed from generation to generation, promoted the progress of human civilization, and contributed greatly to the prosperity and development of the countries along the Silk Road . . . In the 21st century, a new era marked by the theme of peace, development, cooperation, and mutual benefit, it is all the more important for us to carry on the Silk Road Spirit in face of the weak recovery of the global economy, and complex international and regional situations.[2]

China has recently proposed an initiative it calls "One Belt, One Road" to build transport, communications, and energy infrastructure to connect the various regions of Asia, and Asia with Europe. One important group of beneficiaries will be the regions lying between Western Europe and East Asia, including much of Russia and Central Asia. The new infrastructure will link these middle-Eurasian countries more effectively with both Western Europe and East Asia. Some of the key Belt and Road Initiative (BRI) corridors are shown in figure 4.1.

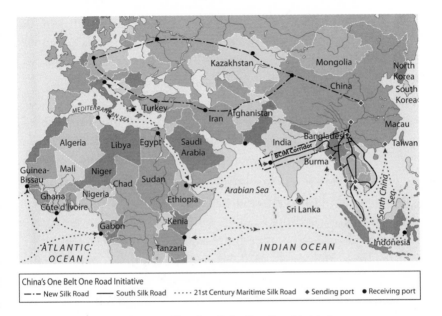

China's One Belt One Road Initiative
—·— New Silk Road ——— South Silk Road ····· 21st Century Maritime Silk Road ◆ Sending port ● Receiving port

FIGURE 4.1 The One Belt, One Road initiative

Source: "China's One Belt One Road Initiative" [map], http://www.eastbysoutheast.com/wp-content/uploads/2015/04/One-Belt-One-Road.png.

The terms "belt" and "road" are a bit counterintuitive. The word "belt" refers to land-based infrastructure such as roads, rail, optical fiber, and power transmission lines, while the word "road" refers to sea routes and seaports. For both the land belts and the sea roads, China's initiative aims to build linkages both within Asia and between Asia and Europe.

Global warming will probably add another important sea route between East Asia and Western Europe, the so-called Northeast Passage in the Arctic Ocean, north of Russia and Norway. With the sea ice disappearing from the Arctic Ocean for more months per year, sea-based trade between East Asia and Europe will be increasingly rerouted from the Indian Ocean and Suez Canal to the Northeast Passage.

This will cut shipping distances by around 25 percent and shipping times by up to half. The Northeast Passage is not an argument for global warming, which will create huge losses overall, but it is a likely beneficial effect among many large negative impacts.

China has not only put forward this new infrastructure vision, but has also put forward new institutional mechanisms to finance it. The most important of these is the new Asian Infrastructure Investment Bank, or AIIB, established by China to cofinance Asia's infrastructure and capitalized by the bank members at $100 billion. Fifty-two countries, including countries of both Europe and Asia, have become members of the bank, and another eighteen are in the queue to join. The United States and Japan have held back, but this hasn't slowed the rest of Europe and Asia (and recently Canada) from signing up. In 2014, China also invested $40 billion in a Silk Road Fund dedicated to financing One Belt, One Road projects.

In addition to the investment funding, China is also promoting new trade and investment agreements. These include the Regional Comprehensive Economic Partnership, a proposed sixteen-country free-trade agreement that would include China, the ten countries of Southeast Asia, and Australia, India, Japan, Korea, and New Zealand.

While Trump is busy proclaiming America First and growling at other countries for their supposed abuses toward the United States, China is making a massive diplomatic and negotiating effort to build trust, trade, investment, and goodwill among the countries of Europe and Asia, not to mention Africa, which China also targets in several investment initiatives. And while there are, of course, widespread concerns that China's initiatives are in the service of China's rising global power, at least China is putting real money on the table—hundreds of billions of dollars of development finance—to build infrastructure of enormous value to the partner economies.

The Chinese government has explained its outward-oriented vision in the following terms:

> The world economic integration is accelerating and regional cooperation is on the upswing. China will take full advantage of the existing bilateral and multilateral cooperation mechanisms to push forward the building of the Belt and Road and to promote the development of regional cooperation. . . . The Belt and Road cooperation features mutual respect and trust, mutual benefit and win-win cooperation, and mutual learning between civilizations. As long as all countries along the Belt and Road make concerted efforts to pursue our common goal, there will be bright prospects for the Silk Road Economic Belt and the 21st-Century Maritime Silk Road, and the people of countries along the Belt and Road can all benefit from this Initiative.[3]

China's emphasis on the win-win character of strengthened trade and investment is reminiscent of language that the United States once used in its more internationalist phase. In 1962, for example, President John F. Kennedy called for a major expansion of trade between the United States and Europe in similar terms: "a freer flow of trade across the Atlantic will enable the two giant markets on either side of the ocean to impart strength and vigor to each other, and to combine their resources and momentum to undertake the many enterprises which the security of free peoples demands." In the event, Kennedy's 1962 call to expand trade led to the signing five years later of the 1967 "Kennedy Round" of multilateral trade liberalization, one of several in which the United States was the vigorous proponent of an open multilateral trading system.

The closer integration of Europe and Asia is an important and logical step in Eurasia's continued economic development. It could also be key to the transition by both Europe and Asia to low-carbon energy systems, if the One Belt, One Road infrastructure is built to promote access to renewable energy through long-distance transmission lines; low-carbon transport via advanced technologies for vehicles, rail, and shipping; and energy efficiency through ubiquitous Internet-based smart systems. Notably, China's industrial strategy aims for major technological advances in all of these areas by the mid-2020s, and BRI investment projects will provide a huge market for these advanced technologies.

One of the remarkable international technology projects now promoted by China is called the Global Energy Interconnection Cooperation and Development, or GEIDCO. The idea is to support rapid decarbonization on a global scale by connecting the world's high-quality renewable energy sources—wind, hydro, solar—through long-distance ultra-high-voltage (UHV) direct-current transmission lines. In GEIDCO's neat formula, the solution to decarbonization is "Smart Grid + UHV Grid + Renewable Energy." Figure 4.2 shows a schematic map of possible interconnections within Asia. GEIDCO has signed up universities, utilities, and power-equipment manufacturers as partners throughout the world.

Each announcement by Trump against global trade, and each accusation by Trump directed at the European Union or China, has pushed these two giants toward each other in a warmer embrace. German Foreign Minister and Vice-Chancellor Sigmar Gabriel recently put it this way:

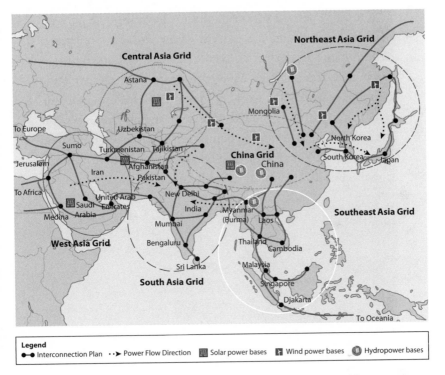

FIGURE 4.2 Proposed Asia grid interconnections for renewable energy

Source: Haibin Wan, *Connotation of Global Energy Interconnection and Asian Grid Interconnection* (Global Energy Interconnection Development and Cooperation Organization, September 2016), https://www.renewable-ei.org/images/pdf/20160908/Wan_Haibin_GlobalEnergyInterconnections.pdf, 14.

(Trump's protectionism) will be very expensive for Americans—the economy doesn't run on pressure and orders from politicians. For Europe, I see opportunities if Trump distances himself not just from China, but all of Asia. Europe should quickly come up with a new Asia strategy. We need to exploit the spaces America is opening up now.[4]

Taken together, Eurasia's economy and population are both around 70 percent of the world, while America's share is now at around 16 percent of world output (down from 22 percent in 1980) and around 4.4 percent of the world's population. Trump may fancy America as still calling the shots, but that era is over. Eurasia will likely constitute the new dynamic center of gravity of the world economy. Both Europe and Asia remain hopeful of continued open trade and investments with the United States, but the countries of Eurasia will not agree to an America First agenda that breaks the rules of the international economy for America's purported advantage.

5

RUSSIA–U.S. RELATIONS IN THE CHANGING WORLD ORDER

While Europe and Asia grow closer, the United States is retrenching along old battle lines. In the view of much of the U.S. security establishment, post-Soviet Russia remains America's biggest security threat. Vladimir Putin, they say, longs to reestablish the Soviet Union, or failing that, at least the Russian Empire, with Russia's wars in Georgia (2008) and in Ukraine (2014), its intervention in Syria after 2014, and its diabolical meddling in the U.S. 2016 election all signs of Russia's ruthless aggression. We have entered a New Cold War—or so we are told.

How far, sadly, we have come from Mikhail Gorbachev's vision of a unified, peaceful, and integrated European home that extended from the North Sea in the west to the Pacific Ocean in Russia's Far East. I believe that we should not give up on that brighter vision. We should understand, indeed, that it was U.S. misguided actions at least as much as Russia's renewed aggression that led us from Gorbachev's vision of a common European home to the new Cold War today.

I know. I watched many of the mistakes close at hand.

To understand Gorbachev's vision, we must go back to the age of the Romanov tsars, part of Europe's Age of Empire.

While the Western European powers expanded into Africa and Asia, European Russia expanded its empire into its near neighborhood in Eastern Europe, Western Asia, and Central Asia. Russia became the largest land empire in the world (although it was rebuffed as a naval power after losing its warm-water port at Sevastopol in the Crimean War with Britain and France).

Russia's industrialization came late compared with Western Europe, part of the general pattern by which European industrialization diffused gradually from west to east during the nineteenth century, yet Russia still had the means to extend its power relative to the weaker and more sparsely populated regions of Central Asia. Russia's expansionism generated conflicts with other European powers and nationalist movements in Eastern Europe, the Balkans, and Western Asia, and with an expansionist Japan in Russia's Far East.

Russian industrial growth picked up in the decade before World War I, but like the other empires of Europe, the Romanov empire was brought down by the war, with the Bolsheviks seizing power in 1917, winning a brutal civil war, and establishing the Soviet Union in 1923. Until World War II, the Soviet Union pursued "socialism in one country," under the increasingly brutal totalitarian regime led by Josef Stalin. In 1939, the Soviet Union disgracefully agreed with Nazi Germany to divide up Poland, only to be invaded by Germany two years later. The Soviet Union bore the brunt of Europe's land war, suffering 20 million military casualties and 20 million more civilian deaths before marching into Berlin in May 1945.

The Cold War followed quickly after. In the predominant U.S. view, the Cold War occurred for one reason and one reason only: the persistent attempt by the Soviet Union to gain control over postwar Western Europe, just as it had over Eastern Europe, and eventually over the world. The United States created NATO to defend against what it viewed as Soviet aggression and expansionism.

Not surprisingly, the view from the Soviet side was somewhat different. From the Soviet perspective, the Soviet Union remained vulnerable to an invasion from the West, as had occurred twice in 150 years, first by Napoleon and second by Hitler. The Soviet Union demanded safety from a resurgent Germany, while the United States was more intent on reviving West Germany and remilitarizing it than on solving the Soviet Union's security concerns. Even worse from the Soviet perspective, the United States under Eisenhower flirted with the idea of a nuclear-armed Germany.

I noted earlier that George Kennan, the State Department's Russia expert in the 1940s and the original author of the U.S. containment policy vis-à-vis Soviet expansionism, did not see the Soviet Union as intent on war with the West. He believed that practical solutions could be found to ease Cold War tensions, and notably floated the idea of a neutral (non-NATO), demilitarized, and unified Germany as an answer to the Soviet Union's security concerns. Kennan had no illusions about Russian repression, and Stalin's particularly reprehensible brand of mass repression and killings. Nonetheless, Kennan believed that peaceful coexistence, and even the end of the Cold War, was possible through diplomatic and essentially nonmilitary means.

In line with Kennan's general approach, John F. Kennedy's decision to deprive West Germany of access to NATO's nuclear weapons was a powerful step forward in easing Cold War tensions, as I describe in detail in my book *To Move the World*.[1] Kennedy indeed succeeded in easing Cold War tensions, and in negotiating the Partial Nuclear Test Ban Treaty with his Soviet counterpart Nikita Khrushchev, and this in turn paved the way for the policy of détente under Nixon. The Soviet Union would keep its planned economy and one-party rule, but the two sides would coexist peacefully. Nixon, Ford, and Carter pursued détente, reaching various arms agreements and other treaty arrangements. From the Soviet point of view, Ronald Reagan represented a dangerous throwback to Western aggression vis-à-vis the Soviet Union, not only placing new nuclear weapons systems in Europe but also speaking provocatively of the possibility of war.

Mikhail Gorbachev came to power in 1985 intent on ending the Cold War while reinvigorating the socialist system, promoting the political and economic reform package termed perestroika. Many Americans, and much of the U.S. security apparatus, attributed Gorbachev's reforms to the economic pressures caused by Reagan's renewed arms race. Other observers, myself included, ascribed Gorbachev's efforts to his recognition of the need for deep reforms of the Soviet economy and viewed Reagan's militarism as both unnecessary and dangerously provocative. Yet for U.S. hard-liners, the message of Gorbachev's reforms was just the opposite: if the United States kept up military pressure, the Soviet Union would fold its hand. The hard-liners felt further vindicated when Gorbachev decided in 1989 to allow, indeed encourage, political multiparty democratization in Eastern Europe.

These differences in interpreting the Gorbachev era mattered then and still matter now. The way we understand this history informs our visions for the future. In my view, Gorbachev was pointing to a new order in Europe in which the security needs of Western Europe, Eastern Europe, and the Soviet Union would be met by ending the economic divisions, moving forward with economic and technological integration, and reversing the arms race. In the hard-liners' view, by contrast, renewed armament had worked, and Russia's economic downward spiral in the late 1980s was the opportunity to win the Cold War, sweep Eastern Europe into the NATO security umbrella, and leave Russia to suffer the consequences of decades of its socialist folly and expansionism.

Poland was the first country to install a noncommunist government, in 1989. I became economic adviser to the government that same year. My vision then was that Poland would quickly rejoin the European Community (later renamed the European Union) as a "normal" mixed economy and democracy, as indeed occurred when Poland joined the European Union in 2004. I wrote the first plan on how the economic transformation could be made to enable Poland's "return to Europe."[2] I saw Poland's steps as the forerunner of Russia's similar reforms. I very much believed in Gorbachev's purpose and vision, that a shared economic space could extend from Rotterdam in the west to Vladivostok in the east.

In 1990 and 1991, I tried to help Gorbachev with a plan similar to Poland's. Poland was receiving timely financial assistance from the United States and other Western nations, and I expected the same to be available to the Soviet Union. Such assistance would need to include a "standstill" on Soviet debt payments; an eventual write-off (cancellation) of part of the Soviet debt to the West; and ample grants from the West, as in the Marshall Plan, to help the Soviet Union rebuild and modernize its economy on market principles.

In the spring of 1991, I worked with Gorbachev's economic adviser Grigory Yavlinsky and with colleagues at Harvard and MIT to prepare a "Grand Bargain," in which the Soviet Union would receive significant funding ($30 billion per year) to restructure its economy, while undertaking political reforms and democratization. The plan was quickly shot down by the White House in the summer of 1991. Gorbachev made a fervent and detailed appeal to the West for economic partnership and support at the G7 Summit in London in July 1991. When this appeal failed, Gorbachev returned home to a coup attempt in August. Russia and the other republics gained political ascendance, and the Soviet Union went into a vertiginous collapse, finally disbanding peacefully in December 1991.

By September, Russian president Boris Yeltsin was reaching out to me and others to help mobilize urgent financial support from the West. Yet this too was not to be. Every recommendation that I made to the White House and the IMF was immediately and decisively shot down. There would be no standstill on debt servicing; there would be no fund to stabilize the currency; there would be no package of assistance for restructuring; there would be no debt reduction. For Poland, yes. For Russia, nyet.

It's hard to know, before the White House, State Department, and Pentagon archives are eventually opened to historians, the exact motivations for America's rejection of basic financial support measures for Russia. The simplest theory is that U.S. support for Eastern Europe was politically popular in the United States (especially given the number of Polish-Americans, Hungarian-Americans, and other hyphenated groups) while support for Russia was not. Another simple theory is confusion: that George H. W. Bush did not really understand the economic and financial challenges facing Russia. Yet perhaps the most realistic theory is that the countries in Eastern Europe were viewed by American strategists and political leaders as possible new NATO members, while Russia was viewed as the continuing enemy, on the other side of the continued divide. In essence, the problem was one of imagination: thinking of Russia as a partner and even ally was just too hard for American leaders steeped in Cold War thinking.

Without access to the help that had so aided Poland and other Eastern European nations, Russia's crisis turned into a rout. Russia ran out of reserves, so the central bank printed rubles to address critical imbalances. The West failed to provide assistance. Inflation soared. Russia's reformers, and their advisers (including myself), took the blame. My deep frustration was to watch Russia sink deeper into crisis while the United States and Europe stood by, immobile, impassive, and unreactive.

Uncontrolled crises go from bad to worse. Quack theories abound. Political discontent multiplies. Reform measures are discredited. Crooks take the places of reformers. When the presidency passed from George H. W. Bush to Bill Clinton, I had hopes that U.S. support would rally, that the United States would move from impassivity to action. Those hopes were dashed. Clinton was inexperienced, uninterested, and inward looking. After the first year of the Clinton presidency, at the end of 1993, I stepped down from advising the Russian government. My three years of pleading for Western help had come to naught.

For the remainder of the 1990s, the United States remained largely impassive to Russia's long-term development needs, but actively attuned to Russian oil contracts and ways to get rich from them. Russia became the Wild East, a place for American adventurers and con artists to plunder rather than a place to aid. Notorious policy scams, such as Russia's "shares for loans" deal, created a new group of super-rich Russian oligarchs, with the United States looking on or actually joining in the scrum. By 1998, the edifice of shambolic financing and privatization tumbled in on itself, with Russia succumbing to the global financial crisis that had started in East Asia in 1997 and later spread to Russia.

When Vladimir Putin succeeded Boris Yeltsin in 2000, Putin still expressed the hope for improved relations with the United States and Europe. Yet the following decade would poison the well. The U.S. lack of assistance to Russia in the early 1990s had been the first snub. American complicity in the rise of the oligarchs was the second grievance. The third cause of rupture was U.S. military policy, notably the expansion of NATO to the East and increased U.S. meddling in the Middle East.

When Gorbachev gave the green light to German reunification in 1990, he reached an explicit agreement with NATO that it would not expand into the territory of East Germany. The spirit of the agreement, according to Gorbachev, was that NATO would not expand to the east, but Gorbachev did not get that in writing. Indeed, Gorbachev later declared that the idea of NATO's eastward expansion did not come up in detail because it was not realistically under consideration or foreseen in 1990. Yet that changed with the dissolution of the Soviet Union. Rather than declaring NATO passé, as it was created in the first place to defend against a Soviet invasion of Western Europe, the United States and its NATO allies took the opportunity to move NATO's military alliance eastward toward Russia.

The expansion of NATO toward the Russian borders is shown in the map in figure 5.1. In 1999, NATO welcomed the Czech Republic, Hungary, and Poland as new members. That might have been acceptable to Russia, but it was followed by several more gulps. In 2004, NATO added Bulgaria, Estonia, Latvia, Lithuania, Romania, Slovakia, and Slovenia as

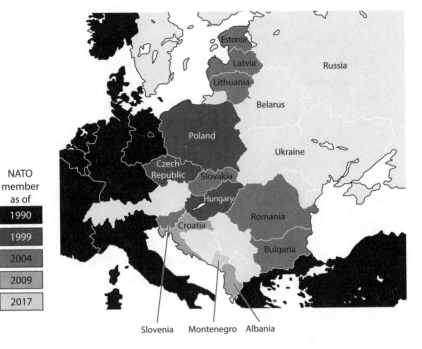

FIGURE 5.1 Map of NATO enlargement, 1949–2017

Source: "Enlargement of NATO," *Wikipedia*, https://en.wikipedia.org/wiki/Enlargement_of_NATO.

members. Putin was irate, asking at the 2007 Munich Security Conference: "Against whom is this [NATO] expansion intended? And what happened to the assurances our Western partners made after the dissolution of the Warsaw Pact?"[3]

But worse was to come. Against the advice and wishes of some NATO members, President George W. Bush decided in 2008 to offer NATO membership to Georgia and Ukraine. This offer, I believe, crossed Putin's red line. Georgia is Russia's immediate neighbor in the underbelly of the Caucuses. Ukraine lies directly athwart Europe and Russia; it is a vital buffer against European invasion, home to Russia's Black Sea naval port, and vital hub of Russia's military industry. The idea that either Georgia or Ukraine would join NATO was unacceptable to Putin. I imagine he saw it as akin to an American president's view were Mexico or Canada invited by China to join a military alliance.

Here again it's helpful to recall the security dilemma. While NATO portrays itself as a defense alliance and claims that Russia has nothing to fear from NATO enlargement, to believe that Russia also sees things this way is utterly naïve. What might look defensive to NATO surely looks offensive to Russia, especially as NATO continues to deploy new weapons systems that Russia finds threatening, to engage in new overseas missions such as the NATO-led overthrow of Libya's Moammar Khadafy in 2011, and to expand to new countries. Albania and Croatia joined in 2009, and Montenegro in 2017.

Russia countered the push toward NATO enlargement with wars in Georgia (2008) and Ukraine (2014); I don't think these two Russian wars, hundreds of miles apart, were coincidental; they were triggered by the prospect that these two countries, right on Russia's borders and deeply intertwined with Russia's economic and security interests, would suddenly become members of NATO. Were Ukraine to join NATO and the European Union, Russia's military base in Sevastopol, on the Crimean Peninsula, would flip into NATO hands. In the end, Putin's actions stopped the advance of NATO to these countries, but not the intention in the minds of American exceptionalists. The tensions with Russia, now including Western sanctions against the Russian economy and the Putin regime, remain very high. Putin, in turn, raised the stakes significantly by Russia's meddling in the 2016 U.S. election.

U.S. policies in the Middle East after 2001 further inflamed the tensions. According to former NATO commander Wesley Clark, America's wars in the Middle East have been designed, in part, to deprive Russia of influence and friendly regimes in Iraq, Syria, and Libya. Putin repeatedly railed against America's regime-change tactics, regarding them as directly destabilizing to the Middle East, hostile to Russia's interests in the region, and a potential forerunner of similar actions by the United States against Russia itself.

By now the situation has become one of almost nonstop tit-for-tat retaliation. U.S. actions spur Russian counteractions, which in turn spur further American responses such as sanctions against the Russian regime, followed by further Russian responses such as cyber-meddling in the 2016 U.S. elections. Trust has disappeared, hard-liners on both sides call for escalation, and recriminations fly in both directions. Americans claim that Putin is trying to recreate the Russian Empire; Putin claims that the United States is trying to establish military dominance over Russia. Hard-liners on one side point to the hard-liners on the other for their proof.

The real solution to this spiraling conflict is to retrace our steps to Gorbachev's vision. There is no fundamental reason why economic cooperation and demilitarization could not stretch from the Atlantic to the Pacific across Russia and Central Asia. Indeed, the rise of China makes this more likely. Russia stands to benefit from the growing economic integration of Eurasia. As China recognizes, cooperation across Eurasia would indeed benefit all parts of the Eurasian landmass. Europe, Russia, China, India, and other parts of Eurasia could work together to connect renewable energy, telecommunications, transport grids, watershed management, environmental protection, and other infrastructure and services. These are all areas of potential massive mutual gain.

While the United States doubles down on its exceptionalist foreign policy—indeed, pushing for an exceptionalism ever

more extreme, with its strains of protectionism and racism—
the rest of the world is recognizing the promise of an internationalist approach. We can learn the hard way by staying the
current course and falling further and further behind. Or we
can embrace a new foreign policy with sustainable development at its heart. The first step in doing so will be to disentan-
gle ourselves from unnecessary wars and break our addiction
to regime change, matters I'll turn to in part II.

Part II

AMERICA'S WARS

It has required our finest historians, such as John Coatsworth and Harry S. Strout, to remind us that U.S.-led "regime change" has been a central pillar, perhaps the defining feature, of American foreign policy for centuries. Outstanding pundits and analysts such as Andrew Bacevich and Stephen Kinzer have filled in much of the detailed and often shocking narrative. Americans like to think of themselves as a peaceful society, but in truth America has been relentlessly at war from the very founding of the first colonies to the present day.

As the world's richest and most powerful nation, America has pursued a foreign policy based on the forcible overthrow of regimes deemed by U.S. security officials and politicians to be hostile to U.S. public or private interests. The CIA, established in 1947 as both an intelligence agency and a secret army for the U.S. president, has been involved in dozens of regime-change interventions, often leading to chaos, and rarely leading to the ostensible purpose: a stable government that is friendly to

U.S. interests. Even when that goal is seemingly achieved in the short run, such as the U.S. and U.K. "successful" overthrow of the elected Iranian government in 1953, after which the United States installed the Shah of Iran, the anti-U.S. blowback came violently and relentlessly a quarter century later with the Iranian Revolution.

America's attention has focused on different regions of the world in different generations. During the first half of the twentieth century, the United States was engaged in both world wars, but also in countless military interventions and regime-change operations in Latin America. These contributed to regional instability, failures of economic reform, and eventually to the anti-American Cuban Revolution that followed decades of U.S. militarism, corruption, and high-handedness vis-à-vis Cuba. In the 1950s to 1970s, America's foreign policy attention focused mainly on Southeast Asia, with the wars and bloodletting in Cambodia, Laos, and Vietnam. In the 1960s to 1980s, the United States once again intervened heavily in Latin America, fomenting military coups and destabilization operations such as the Contra wars in Central America in the mid-1980s.

Since 1979, America's warmaking attention has focused predominantly on the Muslim Middle East, West Asia, and Central Asia. The United States has been engaged in almost nonstop violence in the region since the CIA began to insinuate jihadist forces into Afghanistan, in a successful gambit to provoke a Soviet invasion of that country. Since the Afghanistan war in the 1980s, America has fought two wars in Iraq, supported Iraq in its 1980s war against Iran, supported the Israeli military in several conflicts, and then after the terrorist attacks of 9/11, launched invasions of Afghanistan in 2001 and Iraq in 2003. The United States was also in the forefront of NATO's attack on Libya's Moammar Khadafy in 2011 and Syria's Bashar al-Assad from 2011 until today.

America's wars in the Middle East have had several overlapping motives: oil interests, Israel's strategic interests, U.S. and Saudi opposition to Iranian and Russian influence in the region, and others. Yet the overriding lesson is that these wars are failing to solve deeper political crises, but are leading to calamitous losses of life, property, culture, and well-being.

In this section, I describe the dangers of U.S. exceptionalism based on wars of choice and violent regime change. Such a foreign policy is contrary to the UN Charter and in violation of international law. On a practical level, it often leads to terrorism, instability, and war. My main conclusion is that the U.S. military should withdraw from the region as it finally did successfully and prudently from Southeast Asia in the 1970s and Central America in the 1980s.

In the case of North Korea, that country's fears of U.S.-led regime change are a major impetus to North Korea's development of nuclear weapons and ballistic-missile delivery systems. Without prudence and caution, the ensuing escalation with North Korea could lead to nuclear Armageddon. Unfortunately, Trump's new National Security Strategy points to a continuation of U.S. hubris, a lack of attention to global diplomacy, and the risk of a costly arms race that could spill over into more open conflict.

6

AMERICAN IMPERIALISM AND "WARS OF CHOICE"

American imperialism has always existed hand-in-hand with American exceptionalism. Since the idea of manifest destiny took hold in the nineteenth century, the United States has looked to expand its presence and its influence not just from shore to shore, but also to nations around the world. Viewing America as an empire—and by "empire" I mean a state that uses force to impose rulers on another country—we can better understand that the many wars and conflicts we now find ourselves embroiled in are not wars of necessity, but of choice.

Perhaps the most distinctive characteristic of the American empire is that it was a latecomer to imperial rule. While the European powers, especially Britain and France, were building their far-flung overseas empires in the nineteenth century, the United States was still engaged in its genocidal wars against Native Americans and its Civil War. America's overseas empire building began almost like clockwork in the 1890s, once the United States finally stretched from coast to coast, thereby "closing the frontier" in North America. The next step was overseas empire.

As a latecomer empire, the United States repeatedly found itself taking up the imperial cloak from a former European imperial power. President William McKinley took America to war against Spain in 1898, grabbing Puerto Rico, Cuba, and the Philippines. It did so in the name of supporting local freedom fighters against the Spanish Empire, only to betray those freedom fighters immediately by installing U.S.-backed regimes (in Cuba) or direct rule (in Puerto Rico and the Philippines). McKinley annexed Hawaii the same year, against the wishes of most native Hawaiians.

From 1898 until the end of World War II, the United States had few prospects for expanding its imperial reach, since the British and French empires were still expanding—most notably, after World War I, into the Middle East. But World War II bled Europe dry. Though Britain was a victor in the war, and France was liberated, neither country had the economic, financial, military, or political wherewithal to hold onto their overseas empires, especially since freedom movements in their colonies were engaged in terrorism and guerilla warfare to gain their independence. Britain and France peacefully granted independence to some of their colonies but in other cases fought bloody wars against the independence movements (as the French did in Algeria and Vietnam), almost always losing in the end.

After World War II, the United States asserted global leadership, including through indirect rule. Empires are most visible when they rule directly through conquest and annexation, such as in the U.S. conquests of Hawaii, the Philippines, and Puerto Rico at the end of the nineteenth century. Yet empires also rule indirectly, when they use force, covert or overt, to depose a government they deem hostile and replace it with a government of their design that they intend to keep under their control. Indirect rule—and especially regime-change tactics—has been the more typical U.S. approach. There are dozens of cases in which the CIA or the U.S. military has overthrown governments in Latin America, Asia, Africa, and the Middle East, with the aim of indirect rule.

America's postwar empire building coincided with the Cold War. More often than not, the United States justified its overseas wars and CIA-led coups as necessary to defend itself and its allies against the Soviet Union. American leaders shunned the language of empire and direct rule. Yet the simple fact is that the United States very often had its own narrow interests at heart: oil wealth in the Middle East (such as Iran, 1953); valuable farmlands and industry in Latin America (such as Guatemala, 1954); and U.S. military bases across the world.

The United States often found itself fighting a continuation of earlier imperial wars. Vietnam is a clear case in point. Following World War II, Vietnamese freedom fighters under Ho Chi Minh battled French imperial rule to establish an independent Vietnam. When the Vietnamese defeated the French in a key battle in 1954 and France decided to withdraw, the United States stepped into the fight against the Vietnamese independence fighters, a costly and bloody war that lasted until the U.S. withdrawal in 1975. By that point, more than a million Vietnamese had died at U.S. hands and more than 50,000 American soldiers had lost their lives for no reason. The U.S. warmaking also spread disastrously to neighboring Laos and Cambodia.

In the Middle East, the United States also took up the preceding wars of imperial Britain and France. America's motives were essentially the same: to secure Mideast oil and to project military power in Western Asia, the Eastern Mediterranean, and the Indian Ocean. In 1953, the CIA teamed up with Britain's MI6 to overthrow the elected government of Iran in order to secure Iran's oil for Britain and the United States (another instance of indirect rule). This was Britain's last imperial hurrah in the region, as the United States took the lead from that point onward.

While there are select examples of war ushering in peace— America's shining nobility in World War II and its positive, though flawed, role in the Korean War—we should not let this obscure America's many disastrous wars of choice, when the United States went to war for terrible reasons and ended up causing havoc at home and abroad. Take President Lyndon Johnson's escalation of the war in Vietnam in 1964, done mainly to protect himself against right-wing charges that he was "weak on communism."

Empires trapped in regional wars can choose to fight on or more wisely acknowledge that the imperial adventure is both futile and self-destructive. King George III was wise to give up in 1781; fighting the Americans wasn't worth the effort, even if it was possible militarily. The United States was wise to finally give up the war in Cambodia, Laos, and Vietnam in 1975. America's decision to cut its losses saved not only Southeast Asia but the United States as well. The United States was similarly wise to curtail its CIA-led coups throughout Latin America, as a prelude to peace in the region.

And yet the United States is now ensnared in a perpetual, indeed expanding Middle East war. To examine the political histories of Lebanon, Iraq, Iran, Afghanistan, Syria, Libya, Yemen, and Israel-Palestine after 1950 is to observe the United States engaged in the intrigues, wars, CIA-led coups, and military overthrows that had been the handiwork of Britain and France during earlier decades. The CIA toppled governments in the Middle East on countless occasions. When lamenting the entrenched conflict in the region, media pundits tended to overlook the U.S. role in this instability.

President George W. Bush took America to war against the Taliban-led government of Afghanistan in 2001 and against Iraq's Saddam Hussein in 2003, according to the remarkably naïve neoconservative game plan to rid the greater Middle East of regimes hostile to U.S. interests. The American imperial vision proved to be a fantasy, and the U.S.-led violence came to naught—worse than naught—in terms of U.S. interests.

The issue is not whether an imperial army can defeat a local one. It usually can, just as the United States did quickly in Afghanistan and in Iraq. The issue is whether it gains anything by doing so. Following such a "victory," the imperial power faces unending heavy costs in terms of policing, political instability, guerilla war, and terrorist blowback.

There are also countless bloody cases in which the United States and local allies tried and failed to overthrow a government and instead fomented a prolonged war. The ongoing war in Syria is a case in point.

Our intervention in Syria in support of a rebellion against Bashar al-Assad was ostensibly done on humanitarian grounds. Yet we know from WikiLeaks and other sources that U.S. strategists were looking for a way to topple Assad for years before 2011, hoping that economic instability and IMF-backed austerity would do the job. The United States and Saudi Arabia wanted him out because of Iran's backing of the regime. When the Arab Spring erupted in early 2011, the Obama administration seized on it as an opportunity to nudge Assad out the door.

When Assad showed his staying power, President Obama ordered the CIA to coordinate efforts with Saudi Arabia and Turkey to defeat the regime through support for anti-regime fighters on the ground. Thus, the quick exit of Assad once dreamed of by U.S. strategists turned into a full-blown regional war, with the United States, Saudi Arabia, Turkey, Russia, and Iran all competing for power through proxy fighters including jihadist groups. With backing from Iran and Russia, Assad could not be removed.

The U.S.-led intervention in Libya was also allegedly for humanitarian purposes, to protect civilian populations against Moammar Khadafy. While Khadafy was eventually toppled, his removal required a NATO-led war over several months and, as in Syria, the civilian population ended up suffering horrific harms. Whether the overthrows have succeeded or failed, the long-term consequences have almost always been violence and instability.

The United States is now ensnared in a perpetual, indeed expanding Middle East war, with drones and air strikes increasingly replacing ground troops. In the past, U.S. ground troops committed atrocities, such as My Lai in Vietnam, that were seared into the national conscience. Now that we have drone strikes and bombing runs (as in Syria and Yemen), most of the killings are out of sight, beyond the media's reach. In any event, the U.S. public is completely habituated to war. The U.S. destruction of hospitals, wedding parties, or prayer meetings with dozens or hundreds of civilian casualties hardly registers a moment's notice.

The United States is trapped in the Middle East by its own pseudo-intellectual constructions. During the Vietnam War, the "domino theory" claimed that if the United States withdrew from Vietnam, communism would sweep Asia. The new domino theory is that if the United States were to stop fighting in the Middle East, Islamic terrorists such as ISIS would soon be at our doorstep.

The truth is almost the opposite. ISIS is a ragtag army of perhaps 30,000 troops in a region in which the large

nations—including Saudi Arabia, Iran, Iraq, and Turkey—
have standing armies that are vastly larger and better
equipped. I argued for years that the regional powers could
easily drive ISIS out of the territories it held in Syria and Iraq
if the regional powers chose to do so, and indeed that proved
to be the case in 2017, when both Iraq and Syria retook ISIS
territory. The U.S. military presence in the Middle East is
actually the main recruiting tool for ISIS and other terrorist
groups. Young people stream into Syria and Iraq to fight the
imperial enemy.

Terrorism is a frequent consequence of imperial wars and
imperial rule. Local populations are unable to defeat the imperial powers, so they impose high costs through terror instead.
Consider the terrorism used by Jewish settlers against the
British Empire and local Palestinians in their fight for Israel's
independence and territory; or Serbian terrorism deployed
against the Hapsburg Empire; or Vietnamese terrorism used
against the French and United States in Vietnam's long war
for independence; or American terrorism, for that matter,
that independence fighters used against the British in America's war of independence.

This is of course not to condone terrorism. Indeed, my point
is to condemn imperial rule and to argue for political solutions
rather than the oppression, war, and terror that come in its wake.
Imperial rulers—whether the British in pre-independence
America, the Americans in Cuba and the Philippines after
1898, the French and Americans in Vietnam, or the United
States in the Middle East in recent decades—foment violent
reactions that destroy peace, prosperity, good governance, and
hope. The real solutions to these conflicts lie in diplomacy and
political justice, not in imperial rule, repression, and terror.

So while our current logic compels us to continue ongoing conflicts in order to avoid the spread of terrorism, we should just avoid wars of choice in the first place. If you doubt that they are "of choice," consider that in these cases—the Spanish-American War, the Vietnam War, and the Mideast wars—the United States attacked the other countries first, not in self-defense, as in World War II. The sinking of the USS *Maine* in Havana Harbor in 1898, most likely caused by an onboard explosion in the ship's coal bunkers, became a cause for war when the sinking was attributed to Spain. Lyndon B. Johnson expanded the war in Vietnam on the pretext that North Vietnam had attacked the USS *Maddox* in the Gulf of Tonkin, but Johnson knew that the claim was false. Nor had Saddam, Assad, or Khadafy attacked the United States. The claim that Khadafy was about to commit genocide against his people was propaganda. In the case of Iraq, the pretext was Saddam's nonexistent weapons of mass destruction.

Since the birth of the United Nations in 1945, such wars of choice are actually against international law. The UN Charter allows for wars of self-defense and military actions agreed upon by the UN Security Council. The UN Security Council may approve military interventions to protect civilian populations from the crimes of their own government under the doctrine of "Responsibility to Protect." No country can go it alone other than in self-defense.

Many Americans dismiss the UN Security Council on the grounds that Russia will veto every needed action. Yet this is absolutely not the case. Russia and China indeed agreed to a military intervention in Libya in 2011 in order to protect Libya's civilian population. But then NATO used that UN resolution as a pretext to actually topple Khadafy, not merely to protect the civilian population. Russia and China also recently teamed up with the United States to achieve the nuclear agreement with Iran, to adopt the Paris Climate Agreement, and to adopt the Sustainable Development Goals. Diplomacy is feasible. Getting one's way all the time is not.

There's a good reason such wars are illegal: they have been disasters, one after the next. In the Spanish-American war, the United States gained an empire and fertile farmland in Cuba, but also decades of political instability there and in the Philippines, eventually resulting in Philippine independence and an anti-American revolution in Cuba. In World War I, the U.S. intervention turned the tide toward the victory of France and the United Kingdom over Germany and the Ottoman Empire, only to be followed by a disastrous peace settlement, instability in Europe and the Middle East, and the rise of Hitler in the ensuing chaos fifteen years later. In Vietnam, the war led to 55,000 Americans dead, 1 million or more Vietnamese killed, genocide in next-door Cambodia, destabilization of the U.S. economy, and, eventually, complete U.S. withdrawal.

In Afghanistan, Iraq, and Libya, the regimes were quickly defeated by U.S.-led forces, but peace and stability proved elusive. All of these countries have been wracked by continuing war, terrorism, and U.S. military engagement. And in Syria, the United States was not even successful in toppling Assad—and led to the entry of ISIS into Syria.

It's not so hard to rev up the American public to fight a war, even a horribly misguided one, if the government claims falsely that the United States is under attack or is acting in the service of some grand humanitarian cause. Yet these have been the pretexts, not the reasons, for the wars of choice.

There is one foreign policy goal that matters above all the others, and that is to keep the United States out of a new war, whether in Syria, North Korea, or elsewhere. In 2017 alone, President Trump struck Syria with Tomahawk missiles, bombed Afghanistan with the most powerful nonnuclear bomb in the U.S. arsenal, and sent an armada toward nuclear-armed North Korea. We could easily find ourselves in a rapidly escalating war, one that could pit the United States directly against nuclear-armed countries of China, North Korea, and Russia.

Such a war, if it turned nuclear and global, could end the world. Even a nonnuclear war could end democracy in the United States, or the United States as a unified nation. Who thought the Soviet Union's war in Afghanistan would end the Soviet Union itself? Which of the belligerents at the start of World War I foresaw the catastrophic end of four giant empires—Hohenzollern (Prussia), Romanov (Russia), Ottoman, and Hapsburg—as a result of the war?

There are actions we can undertake to prevent new wars and covert engagements. As a first step, the CIA should be drastically restructured, to be solely an intelligence agency rather than an unaccountable secret army of the president. When the CIA was created in 1947, it was given the two very different roles of intelligence and covert operations. Truman was alarmed about this dual role, and time has proved him right. The CIA has been a vital success when it provides key intelligence, but an unmitigated disaster when it serves as the president's secret army. We need to end the military functions of the CIA, yet Trump has recently expanded the CIA's war-making powers by giving the agency the authority to target drone strikes without Pentagon approval.

Second, it is vital for Congress to reestablish its decision-making authority over war and peace. That is its constitutional role, indeed perhaps its most important constitutional role as a bulwark of democratic government. Yet Congress has almost completely abandoned this responsibility. When Trump brandishes the sword toward North Korea or drops bombs on Afghanistan, Iraq, Syria, and Yemen, Congress is mute, neither investigating nor granting nor revoking any legislative authority for such actions. This is Congress's greatest dereliction of duty. Congress needs to wake up before Trump launches an impetuous and potentially calamitous war against nuclear-armed North Korea.

Third, it is essential to break the secrecy over U.S. foreign policy-making. Most urgently, we need an inquest into U.S. involvement in Syria in order for the public to understand how we arrived at the current morass. Since Congress is unlikely to undertake this, and since the executive branch would of course never do so, the responsibility lies with civil society, especially academia and other policy experts, to coalesce around an information-gathering and -reporting function.

Fourth, we need urgently to return to global diplomacy within the UN Security Council, as I'll consider further in part IV.

Finally, the United States must get out of those conflicts it's already involved in. This means an immediate end to its fighting in the Middle East and a turn to UN-based diplomacy for real solutions and security. The Turks, Arabs, and Persians have lived together as organized states for around 2,500 years. The United States has meddled unsuccessfully in the region for sixty-five years. It's time to let the locals sort out their problems, without their being inflamed by outside powers, and supported by the good offices of the United Nations, including peacekeeping and peace-building efforts. Just recently, the Arabs once again wisely and rightly reiterated their support for a two-state solution between Israelis and Palestinians if Israel withdraws from the conquered territories. America's unhelpful interventions are sure to fail. As we'll see in the next chapter, the complex history of this region—made all the more complex through foreign meddling—requires that the states involved take the lead. We should support their decisions with diplomacy, not war.

7

ENDING THE ISRAELI-PALESTINIAN CONFLICT

Peace between Jews and Arabs in Israel and Palestine (Gaza and the West Bank) has been elusive for a century. The United States has repeatedly aimed at brokering a peace deal, only to see the negotiations crash in a new round of enmity and violence. When Donald Trump unilaterally recognized Jerusalem as Israel's capital in December 2017, over the strenuous objections of the other UN Security Council members and the UN General Assembly, the Palestinian Authority denounced the United States, abandoned the quarter-century of negotiations under the Oslo Agreement, and asserted that the Palestinians would never allow the United States to play the role of peace mediator again.

The truth is that such enmity has been present ever since the 1917 Balfour Declaration, by which the British Empire declared a Jewish homeland in the Ottoman region of Palestine. When the Ottoman Empire was defeated in World War I and subsequently collapsed, the British Empire took control of Palestine in 1920 and began to implement the Balfour Declaration, admitting Jewish settlers in large numbers into the British mandate. Since then, Arabs and Jews in Palestine (and after 1948, Israel) have clashed repeatedly and remorselessly. As with so many other conflict zones, the European imperial power (in this case Britain) turned the mess over to the United States after World War II. Since then, the United States has claimed to be acting as a broker and mediator between the two parties. In practice, the United States has been the guarantor and financier of Israel's security, and the Palestinians have repeatedly rejected U.S. peace offers as one-sided in favor of Israel.

For the past one hundred years, one can track four positions in the often desperate clash of interests.

The first, held by Arab hard-liners today, is that the Jewish homeland of the Balfour Declaration, and later the state of Israel, are products of European imperialism, specifically the British Empire, and a violation of basic Arab rights. This position calls for an end to the state of Israel, and for the hardest hard-liners the dismantling and departure of the Jewish community.

The second, held by Jewish hard-liners today, is that the Jewish state marks the return of the Jewish people to the state promised them by God. The exile is over, and the Jews have returned to their biblical homeland. The Arabs have no claims to the Jews' God-given lands and should be encouraged to leave the Jewish lands entirely, or at most to live in Jewish-controlled enclaves akin to the Bantustans of apartheid South Africa.

The third, apparently held by majorities of both Jewish Israelis and Arabs, according to countless opinion surveys over several decades, is that the region that was once Ottoman Palestine and later the British Mandatory Region should be divided into two states, Israel and Palestine, living peacefully with each other, with Jerusalem the capital of both countries (Arab-majority East Jerusalem in the case of Palestine). This, of course, is the "two-state solution." The predominant idea, enshrined in UN declarations and the Oslo peace process, is that the division of the two states should occur along the boundaries of Israel before the 1967 war, with minor and mutually agreed small variations.

The fourth, considered a radical and idealistic vision by many or most, is a one-state solution with Jews and Arabs living side by side, with national (ethnic) rights for each community. Just as Belgium is divided between the Flemish and Walloons, the single binational state would be divided between Jews and Arabs.

Depending on one's point of view, then, the Israel-Palestine conflict is (a) a fundamental clash of religious claims, Bible versus Koran; (b) a legacy of European imperialism; or (c) an issue in need of urgent, practical, mutual accommodation. In a real sense, of course, it is all of the above, since there are ardent advocates of each of these perspectives. There is a fourth perspective as well, the politics of regional power. Just as Britain's control of Mandatory Palestine was part of Britain's overarching imperial strategy for the Middle East and the Indian Ocean, America's role in the conflict is part of America's grand strategy as well, a piece of the exceptionalist world map. U.S. exceptionalism has made U.S. mediation ineffective at the least, and duplicitous in practice, failing to insist on the mutual accommodations by both sides that could lead to peace.

As in so many other parts of the Middle East, and indeed other parts of the world, the roots of today's crisis go back to duplicitous dealings by the European imperial powers during and after World War I. Let us therefore return to the situation a century ago, to better understand possible solutions for today and the future.

The lands that today are Israel, Gaza, and the West Bank were over the course of the past 3,000 years parts of the biblical Jewish kingdoms of Israel and Judah, Assyria, Babylonia, Persia, Greek (Selucid) empire, Hasmonean (Jewish) dynasty, Roman empire, Byzantium, various Muslim caliphates, Crusader Kingdom, Egyptian Mamluks, and starting in 1517, the Ottoman Empire for four centuries. During the Ottoman period, the region of Palestine was settled overwhelmingly by Arabs. Small numbers of religious Jews lived in Jerusalem for centuries, and greater numbers of Jewish emigrants began to arrive at the end of the nineteenth century following the anti-Jewish pogroms in Russia. The idea of a renewed Jewish homeland in the Jews' biblical lands was revived at the end of the nineteenth century by Theodor Herzl, the Vienna-based founder of modern Zionism.

During World War I, Britain planned for the postwar takeover of the Ottoman lands, including the lands of Israel and Palestine, which after the war and up to the time of Israel's independence in 1948 would become known as Mandatory Palestine (so named for the League of Nations mandate giving Britain control over the area). British colonial strategists identified four main British interests regarding Ottoman Palestine. The first was to secure the eastern flank of the Suez Canal, which was the British Empire's major trade route to Asia and its lifeline to British India. The second was to secure an Eastern Mediterranean port for Middle East oil, notably for the oil anticipated to come from British-controlled Mosul (now in Iraq). The third was to divide the Mideast spoils with Britain's main wartime ally, France. And the fourth aim was to dangle promises regarding Palestine to other parties in order to gain support for Britain's war effort.

For the fourth purpose, winning the war, Britain promised the land of what would soon become Mandatory Palestine three times over in contradictory commitments. Britain's first promise was the secret 1916 Sykes-Picot Treaty with France to divide the territory between Britain and France. Britain's second promise, in the McMahon-Hussein Correspondence, was to pledge the land to the Arabs in return for their revolt against the Turkish Ottoman overlords. The third promise, the Balfour Declaration, called for the creation of a Jewish homeland in Palestine. The goal, according to historians, was in part to entice the United States to back the British war efforts, and even to entice the Bolshevik leadership (imagined by Britain to be pro-Jewish) to come onside as well.

Not surprisingly, these utterly contradictory commitments gave rise to the unending strife that has now lasted a full century. The world still reels from this remarkable episode of British imperial duplicity. In a similar way, the world still suffers from like-mannered machinations of the British and French regarding the post-Ottoman provinces of today's Lebanon, Iraq, and Syria.

From the moment that World War I ended, the Arabs demanded the fulfillment of the promised reward for their fight against the Turks. Meanwhile, the Jews similarly demanded their homeland in Palestine. The famous Jewish quip that the new Jewish homeland was a "land without a people for a people without a land" was never remotely true. Nor was there ever Arab acquiescence in Britain's diplomatic sleight of hand, promising Arab lands to both Arabs and Jews. The century-long contest between Jews and Arab Palestinians for political control and ownership over the land thus ensued.

During the Mandatory period (1923–1948), during which Britain had administrative control over Palestine and a responsibility of "tutelage" of the region, Britain faced unending difficulties in managing the bitterly conflicting claims of the Jews and Palestinians. Riots, intercommunal violence, and struggles over Jewish immigration to Palestine bedeviled the British mandate. The Arabs bitterly, and largely successfully, resisted Jewish migration, even as Nazism threatened the Jews' very survival in Europe. Jews perished in unimaginable numbers because the immigration route to Palestine was blocked by the British in the face of Arab resistance.

At the end of the World War II, the sentiments of the United Kingdom and the United States were initially for a one-state solution. An Anglo-American Committee of Inquiry in 1946 called for increased Jewish immigration of Holocaust survivors in the context of essentially a single state: "In order to dispose, once and for all, of the exclusive claims of Jews and Arabs to Palestine, we regard it as essential that a clear statement of principle should be made that Jew shall not dominate Arab and Arab shall not dominate Jew in Palestine."[1]

Two years later, in 1947, the newly constituted UN General Assembly passed a nonbinding resolution recommending a two-state solution based on the partition of Palestine between Arabs and Jews, with Jerusalem becoming an international city. The Arab countries, and several others, heatedly rejected this recommendation and instead called for self-determination by the existing population of Palestine, which was predominantly Arab at the time. Britain unilaterally announced that it would end its mandate over Palestine in May 1948, signaling its imminent departure. In the lead-up to Britain's withdrawal from Palestine, President Truman called for a temporary UN trusteeship until the issues of sovereignty could be peacefully resolved.

When Britain's mandate ended, Israel immediately and unilaterally declared its independence and then was victorious in the ensuing war to defend its claim. In the course of the 1948 war, many Arab families fled their homelands and countless others were violently pushed out of their homes through the use of Israeli terror and force. In this way arose the Palestinian refugees who up to today claim the right of return to their homeland in Palestine.

The history therefore shows that the competing claims by the Palestinians and Jews have raged for a century, and that both the one-state and two-state solutions have been tabled at various times. Israel has established "facts on the ground," as it were, to achieve control over most of the territory of mandatory Palestine, part of which is Israel of the 1967 borders and the rest, the territories captured by Israel in the 1967 war.

Practical politicians on both the Israeli and Palestinian sides, and in the United States, have argued for several decades for a two-state solution, based largely on a return by Israel to the borders as they existed before the 1967 Six-Day War, with some agreed border adjustments in Jerusalem and other places. Yet that two-state prospect has failed so far, in no small part because the Israeli government actively encouraged Jewish settlement in the West Bank; Jewish West Bank settlers now number around 400,000 and constitute a very powerful if not decisive force in Israeli politics.

Some analysts have recently argued that the settler position is now so entrenched that a two-state solution has become practically impossible. Others argue that a two-state solution is still possible, though just barely, and that the slim remaining prospects for a two-state solution will soon disappear as the Jewish population in the West Bank continues to grow. As a result, the one-state solution has garnered renewed interest in both its variants: a binational solution and a Jewish-nationalist variant.

A binational one-state solution, similar to the Belgian model, could have practical appeal and viability. The Arab and Jewish communities would be self-governing regarding religion, local policing, family, and other intracommunity law, and broadly speaking, in municipal affairs if one community or the other predominates. There would have to be constitutional agreements on national security, foreign policy, internal migration, and the endlessly knotty issue of the return of Palestinian refugees.

None of this would be easy, but it could be possible. Nothing in the Holy Land has been easy for at least the past 3,000 years. The Middle East is indeed in the middle of competing claims: by religion (Jewish, Christian, Muslim), ethnicity (Arab, Turkish, Persian, Jewish, Druze, Kurd, other), and geopolitics (Iran, Saudi Arabia, Turkey, Russia, the United States, the European Union, and others). Compromise among competing interests is the sine qua non for any kind of peace arrangement.

Hard-liners argue for a very different one-state solution, in which Palestinian political rights would be severely limited. This one-state vision is one of apartheid: Arabs living as second-class citizens under Jewish control. Sensible Israelis and true friends of Israel should understand that most of the world will never accept such a solution, and it would prove deeply corrosive to Israel's democratic norms and the moral code of the Jewish people. It might be possible to impose for a while out of sheer force, but it will lead to hatred, backlash, and political illegitimacy. It cannot be a peaceful equilibrium.

The Israeli government accuses the UN Security Council and UN General Assembly of anti-Israeli virulence. It's true that votes in the UN run strongly against Israel's settlement and occupation policies, but they also run strongly for a peaceful, two-state solution. The UN member states are not so much against Israel as they are against Israel's occupation policies, and the attempt by some Israeli hard-liners to create an apartheid state by annexing lands conquered in 1967, an action that would be starkly in violation of international law. The UN votes against Israeli settlements (as in December 2016) reflect a widely shared interpretation of international law, including the Fourth Geneva Convention of 1949, that bars settlements by an occupying power in territories occupied in war. The adoption in December 2016 by the Knesset (the Israeli parliament) of a law allowing the expropriation of privately owned Palestinian land triggered similar global opprobrium and even the revulsion of mainstream political parties and legal experts in Israel itself.

Trump's unilateral recognition of Jerusalem as the capital of Israel in December 2017 brought about a similar international rebuke of both the United States and Israel (which gleefully but naïvely applauded Trump's move). Under international law and countless decisions by the UN, the final status of Jerusalem should be decided by negotiation, not unilateral action by the United States or Israel. Trump's action was therefore rebuked in the UN Security Council by a vote of 14–1 against the United States, and in the UN General Assembly by a vote of 128 to 9, with 35 abstentions, and that despite a threat by the United States to cut off aid to countries that voted against the U.S. action.

Many Israeli religious hard-liners cite the Jewish belief in God's covenant to the Jewish people promising the land of Israel exclusively to the Jews. Yet such claims are doubly problematic. One obvious difficulty is that conflicting claims by Jews and Arabs based on differing religious convictions result in irreconcilable positions that lead repeatedly to tragedy, suffering, and stalemate rather than peace. Fortunately, the majority of both Jews and Arabs agree on the feasibility of compromise and mutual accommodation, rather than the all-or-nothing, negative-sum struggles envisaged by the religious hard-liners on both sides.

There is another deep reason for worry within the perspective of Jewish belief itself. The Jewish Scriptures, it is argued by many devout Jews, do not demonstrate an unconditional Jewish hold on the lands promised by God to the Jewish people. The great prophetic texts of the Jewish people (for example, in the books of the prophets Hosea, Amos, Jeremiah, and Isaiah) describe how the iniquity of the Jewish kingdoms of Israel and Judah in the days of the First Temple of Jerusalem would eventually lead to their conquest by foreign powers. These great Jewish prophets underscored that the threat to the survival of the Jewish states of those days lay not in the military power of Assyria and Babylonia but in the decline of moral reverence by the Jewish people. The Jewish states, declared the prophets, would be lost because of internal iniquity, not external force.

Those prophetic teachings should resonate today for Israel's closest friends, including the United States. Israel's threats today are not only, or perhaps even mainly, external, for Israel is militarily strong; arguably, the direst threat lies in the weakening of Israel's resilience, unity, and morale if it turns away from the requirements of justice, including toward the Palestinian people. Israelis and Palestinians remain challenged by British actions a century ago: the promise of the same land to two peoples. If a hard-line one-state solution is a moral and practical dead end, and if Israel won't countenance a binational solution, the Israeli government should quickly reinvigorate the two-state solution before it's too late.

Trump's belligerence toward the Palestinians and his unilateral actions in declaring Jerusalem the capital of Israel have only made compromise and trust that much harder to achieve. We will have to clean up after Trump's rash and irresponsible actions as a prelude to a just solution for the peoples of Israel and Palestine.

8

NORTH KOREA AND
THE DOOMSDAY CLOCK

The most chilling concern about Donald Trump is the worldwide fear that he puts our very survival at risk. This is not loose talk or partisanship. It was recently expressed by the most thoughtful experts who monitor the risks to our survival: the Science and Security Board of the *Bulletin of the Atomic Scientists*, who are the keepers of the Doomsday Clock.[1]

On January 26, 2017, just a week after Donald Trump was sworn into office as the new president of the United States, the scientists who orchestrated the clock announced that the world was "Two and a half minutes to midnight," where midnight signifies the end of civilization. They cited Trump's "ill-considered comments about expanding and even deploying the American nuclear arsenal" as well as his "expressed disbelief in the scientific consensus on global warming." A year later, in January 2018, the group inched the clock forward another thirty seconds, just two minutes to midnight—to global catastrophe. This is the closest it has been to midnight since 1953, when the United States and the Soviet Union first exploded the new thermonuclear weapons, powerful enough to end all human life on the planet.

As we see in the timeline in figure 8.1, we are now as close to doom as we were in 1953, when both the United States and Russia first possessed thermonuclear weapons capable of destroying the world. "To call the world's nuclear situation dire is to understate the danger and its immediacy," the *Bulletin* said.

The Doomsday Clock was created seventy years ago, in the early days of the Cold War and the nuclear weapons race between the United States and the Soviet Union. For the first time in human history, mankind possessed the means of causing not only great carnage and suffering, but also the very destruction of humanity. The early generation of atomic scientists recognized the profound and unprecedented dangers

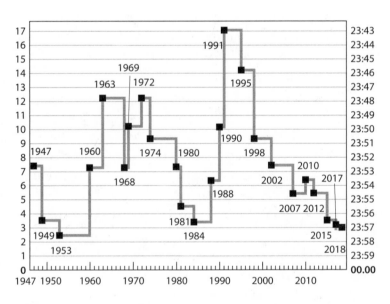

FIGURE 8.1 The Doomsday Clock

Note: Minutes to midnight, 1947–2017

Source: "Doomsday Clock," *Wikipedia*, https://en.wikipedia.org/wiki/Doomsday_Clock.

of the new weapons and sought to warn the world. In the first edition of the clock, in 1947, they set the time to seven minutes before midnight, nuclear Armageddon. As the Cold War intensified, and atomic bombs gave way to vastly more powerful thermonuclear bombs, the minute hand moved five minutes closer to midnight.

When President Kennedy came into office, in his inaugural address he powerfully expressed the existential paradox of modernity: "For man holds in his mortal hands the power to abolish all forms of human poverty and all forms of human life." We never came closer to the end than in the Cuban Missile Crisis of October 1962, when mistakes by both the United States and the Soviet Union led the world to the very brink of nuclear war. Many of the military advisers on Kennedy's Executive Committee would have led us into thermonuclear war. The Kennedy brothers, John and Robert, with their cool heads and profound sense of responsibility, saved us despite their advisers, not because of them. We should all shudder when contemplating an Executive Committee meeting in our time.

Then in 1963, brilliant diplomacy by Kennedy, supported by the moral leadership of Pope John XXIII and the bold statesmanship of Nikita Khrushchev, led to the signing of the Partial Nuclear Test Ban Treaty. Humanity was spared (possibly at great personal cost—some think that right-wingers took such offense to JFK's peace initiative that the president was assassinated as a result; there is real plausibility to that view). The minute hand of the Doomsday Clock moved back to twelve minutes before midnight, a margin of safety.

With America's escalation of the Vietnam War under Lyndon Johnson, the minute hand began to move once again toward midnight, while Richard Nixon's détente with the

Soviet Union again reduced tensions and put the minute hand back to twelve minutes before midnight. Then tensions escalated with Ronald Reagan's new arms buildup, until Soviet president Mikhail Gorbachev launched perestroika, culminating in the end of the Cold War and the end of the Soviet Union itself in 1991. Humanity had, it seemed, reached a moment of relative safety; the minute hand stood that year at seventeen minutes before midnight.

Yet if ever a historic opportunity for safety was squandered, this was it. Every U.S. president since then—Bill Clinton, George W. Bush, and Barack Obama—has contributed to a decline of global safety, with the minute hand moving from seventeen minutes before midnight to just three minutes before midnight last year, even before Donald Trump became president. And after just a few days in office came another thirty-second jump of the minute hand toward midnight.

What went wrong between 1991 and now? Two grave mistakes were made. The first was the failure to capitalize on the end of the Cold War by establishing a trustworthy relationship between the United States and Russia, as detailed in chapter 5. The second mistake was to turn a blind eye to the second existential threat: human-induced global warming. While the danger of nuclear weapons was easy enough to perceive (though also easy to forget day to day), the existential threat from human-induced climate change was far more difficult. To understand it requires at least a basic awareness of quantum physics, the Earth's physical dynamics, and Earth's climate and economic history. Our presidents and Congress have lacked that. They understand money from lobbyists—oil and gas companies—not quantum physics.

There are dire risks associated with our continued burning of coal, oil, and gas. When these fossil fuels are burned, they emit carbon dioxide into the atmosphere. Carbon dioxide has the special quantum-mechanical property that it absorbs infrared radiation and thereby acts as a kind of atmospheric "greenhouse" for Earth, causing the planet to warm. This is of course clear to atmospheric chemists, but not to most politicians. The science and Earth history also make clear that we are recklessly gambling with future survival. The ocean level could rise by twenty feet or more as a result of even slight further increases in temperature. Only a fool would say that because such an outcome is not completely certain, we should simply continue to burn fossil fuels at the maximum rate.

The *Bulletin* made clear that the failure to act on climate change was a major reason for moving the Doomsday Clock forward in 2017, noting that Trump's "nominees to head the Energy Department and the Environmental Protection Agency dispute the basics of climate science." In 2018, moving the minute hand another thirty seconds toward midnight, they wrote: "The nations of the world will have to significantly decrease their greenhouse gas emissions to keep climate risks manageable, and so far, the global response has fallen far short of meeting this challenge."[2]

Trump and his cabinet are in denial. Trump has completely turned his administration's environmental policies over to the oil and gas industry. The State Department is now in the hands of ExxonMobil; the Environmental Protection Agency is in the hands of politicians like Scott Pruitt, long financed by the fossil-fuel industry. The word on Capitol Hill is simple: The mega-billionaire Koch brothers, who own the nation's largest private fossil-fuel company, own Congress, or at least the Republican side.

When it comes to nuclear weapons, the issue is not denial but inconsistency. Trump has casually suggested that Japan and Korea should become nuclear powers; that a new nuclear-arms race is welcome; and that the use of nuclear weapons (e.g., in regard to ISIS) is not "off the table." Yet, for every statement such as these, there are equal and opposite statements as well. There is, in short, casualness, inconsistency, and incoherence.

Trump is impetuous, unstable, and inexperienced. His foreign policies swing wildly from day to day. He makes threats, such as attacking North Korea or conflict with Iran, that could have horrific, indeed catastrophic, consequences. American arrogance and President Donald Trump's delusional worldview have brought the world to the brink of nuclear war. Before it is too late, American citizens must make overwhelmingly clear that we do not want millions of Americans or others to perish in a reckless attempt by the Trump administration to overthrow the North Korean or Iranian regime or denuclearize North Korea by force.

We would rather accept a nuclear-armed North Korea that is deterred by America's overwhelming threat of force than risk a U.S.-led war of choice, one that would almost surely involve nuclear weapons. Yet in 2017, then-National Security Adviser H. R. McMaster explicitly said that Trump rejects "accept and deter." The dangers are exceedingly high.

"Accept and deter" would not be appeasement. Though negotiations and sanctions could conceivably induce the North to relinquish its nuclear weapons, the odds remain low and North Korea's nuclear weapons are likely to remain for many years to come. "Accept and deter" is therefore likely to be the moral and practical requirement of survival. Appeasement would be the case if North Korea were demanding the surrender of the United States or South Korea, but that's not the case. North Korea argues that it needs nuclear arms to protect the regime from the threat of a U.S. attack. According to

North Korea, it seeks a "military equilibrium," not a surrender of the United States or South Korea.

Sad to say, North Korea's fears of a U.S.-led overthrow are realistic from North Korea's perspective. Creating the conditions for North Korea's eventual denuclearization would require trust-building over many years of patient diplomacy and interaction, including U.S. diplomatic recognition of North Korea.

The United States faces a trap of its own making. For decades, this country has forcibly overthrown regimes it deemed hostile to U.S. interests. North Korea fears that it is next.

Wars can happen accidentally, especially in situations like this, when there is so much mistrust, misunderstanding, and inflexible posturing.

Recently, three regimes that ended their nuclear programs were subsequently attacked by nuclear powers. Saddam Hussein's nuclear weapons program came to an end after the first Gulf War, in 1990; Saddam was overthrown by the United States in 2003. Moammar Khadafy ended his nuclear program in December 2003 and was overthrown by U.S.-backed forces in 2011. Ukraine surrendered its nuclear forces in 1994 in return for security guarantees, but was subsequently attacked by Russia in 2014.

Since the early 1990s, North Korea has repeatedly demanded security guarantees from the United States—including diplomatic recognition, economic measures, and other steps—in exchange for ending its drive toward a nuclear arsenal. Several agreements were in fact reached on the idea of guaranteeing North Korean security in return for denuclearization, yet all of the agreements subsequently collapsed. A very insightful and balanced account of these failed attempts is provided in a Brookings Institution report by a senior Chinese foreign policy expert, Fu Ying, chair of the Foreign Affairs Committee of the National People's Congress of China.

Mutual distrust is the basic reason for repeated failures. The United States again and again dragged its feet on granting diplomatic recognition and economic assistance to North Korea, despite explicit promises to do so. North Korea, for its part, violated the spirit if not the letter of the agreements, using covert means at times to skirt agreed nuclear safeguards. Both sides have been trapped in the security dilemma, in which defensive actions by one are seen as offensive by the other. The result is a terrifying arms race and downward spiral toward nuclear war.

In this tit-for-tat pattern, it is difficult if not impossible to identify who has broken the various accords first. The bottom line is that there is no security agreement for North Korea, and no long-term suspension or abandonment by North Korea of its nuclear program. Now Trump's temperamental instability could trigger a nuclear war through the belief adopted by either side that the other is about to launch a devastating preemptive attack. Add to this the human element—errors such as the mistaken alert of a ballistic missile headed for Hawaii in January 2018—and we see again how terrifying prospects that may seem unreal, even preposterous, are utterly possible if we aren't judicious, cautious, and wise. Unfortunately, Trump is the very opposite: rash, impulsive, and ignorant.

The Trump administration has threatened North Korea with war if it fails to denuclearize. Even as Trump has turned from threats to negotiations, there may well be senior U.S. security advisers who believe in the possibility of a quick "decapitation" of the North Korean regime before its nuclear weapons are unleashed. Some advisers may believe that America's anti-missile systems would protect the United States and its allies in the event that North Korea launched its nuclear weapons.

In my view, any confidence in a military solution is reckless and immoral. Most expert assessments suggest massive deaths in South Korea, perhaps 20,000 per day, from a conventional war, much less a nuclear war. Most experts believe that the antimissile systems are highly imperfect, with a real possibility of failure.

If there is one lesson of history, it is to doubt the boastful pronouncements of warmongers. Things go wrong. One's own weapons systems frequently fail. Treachery, surprise, accidents, errors are the essence of war. And with nuclear war, one doesn't get a second chance. During the Cuban Missile Crisis, Kennedy's reckless generals urged a military attack, believing that a nuclear war could be avoided. The truth was that Russian and Cuban troops were already deployed to use battlefield nuclear weapons in the event of a conventional U.S. attack.

Perhaps the most important lesson that came out of the Cuban Missile Crisis is the conclusion of President Kennedy in his famous "Peace Speech" of June 1963, which ushered in the Partial Nuclear Test Ban Treaty:

> Above all, while defending our own vital interests, nuclear powers must avert those confrontations which bring an adversary to a choice of either a humiliating retreat or a nuclear war. To adopt that kind of course in the nuclear age would be evidence only of the bankruptcy of our policy—or of a collective death-wish for the world.[3]

Amen.

Let's not panic. Instead, let's think, plan, and act. To quote Kennedy once more: "Our problems are manmade—therefore, they can be solved by man." The problem of Donald Trump can be solved too, by the institutions of American democracy and the international rule of law.

Trump is a bully whose bluster is designed to intimidate and wrong-foot a foe, and in Trump's worldview, just about everybody is a foe. As he has famously explained, in an attitude inherited from his father, there are "killers" and there are "losers." The bluster is designed to put Killer Trump ahead of the losers. The key to survival in the Trump era is to look past the bluster, face down the bullying, and prevent Trump's poorly controlled emotions from guiding the policies of the United States on these life-and-death issues.

The turn from name-calling to negotiation with North Korea gives some reason for hope, but it is all too easy to see how the spectacle of summits could slide back into acrimony, vitriol, and threats. The US demands denuclearization; North Korea demands security, and there is as yet no evidence that the reciprocal demands have been reconciled. With Trump's instability and lack of attention span, anything can happen.

Trump's impulsiveness will need to be checked. This check will come in part from our courts, which must scrutinize the various poorly prepared and ill-considered executive orders that have come from the administration; many will be quashed. Regulatory agencies must also follow rigorous procedures to change existing regulations, all of which are subject to court review and congressional supervision. Another check could come if a few patriotic Republican senators join with the Democrats to put a stop to Trump's mad rush of recklessness. Will Senators John McCain, Lindsey Graham, Susan Collins, Rob Portman, Lisa Murkowski, or Ron Paul, among others, really stand by if Trump brings us to the brink of nuclear war?

Other checks will come from outside our borders. Trump is rapidly uniting the world—against the United States. Within just two weeks of taking office, Trump had the European Union president listing the Trump administration alongside Russia, China, and the Middle East as threats to the European Union. China's president Xi Jinping has offered to take up the internationalist mantle that Trump is so eager to relinquish. Almost all of the world is also united in urging the handful of nuclear-weapons countries to honor their solemn obligations, under the Nuclear Nonproliferation Treaty, to take concrete steps toward nuclear disarmament, and not to instigate a renewed and dangerous arms race.

Finally, of course, there is electoral politics. In moments of pessimism, it may seem that Trump will trample American democracy, thereby preventing a course correction in 2020 or earlier. Yet Trump is no Caesar or Augustus, and the United States is no republican Rome on the verge of succumbing to dictatorship. No doubt Trump can do great damage; our institutional checks and balances have been gravely weakened by decades of rule by the military-industrial-intelligence complex. Presidents indeed have the power to launch wars, even secret ones run by the CIA and special ops units that can kill vast numbers of innocents. But it's my sincere hope that the American people, and our political institutions, are not ready to accede to bullies.

The United States has developed a level of wealth, productivity, and technological know-how utterly unimaginable in the past. Yet we put everything at risk through our wanton addiction to war. If we instead used our vast knowledge, economic might, and technological excellence to help cure diseases, end poverty, protect the environment, and ensure global food security, America would profoundly inspire other nations and do much to secure a new era of global peace.

Checks on Trump's recklessness and warmongering cannot come soon enough; as we'll see in the next chapter, his emerging ideas about national security and nuclear weapons are a danger to us all.

9

TRUMP'S NEW NATIONAL SECURITY STRATEGY

E very few years, the executive branch produces a National Security Strategy (NSS) to describe the administration's national security priorities and strategies to address them. The Trump administration released its first NSS in December 2017.[1] As with past strategies, the Trump strategy is grounded in a naïve and dangerous U.S. exceptionalism. To fully appreciate these dangers, Trump's NSS should be read alongside the new National Defense Strategy of the United States[2] and Nuclear Forces Posture.[3]

The dominant tone of the Trump-era documents is bleak: the United States faces a world of hostility. Cooperation has failed. Only a renewed military buildup can succeed. The National Defense Strategy is worth quoting at length:

> Today, we are emerging from a period of strategic atrophy, aware that our competitive military advantage has been erod-ing. We are facing increased global disorder, characterized by decline in the long-standing rules-based international order—creating a security environment more complex and volatile than any we have experienced in recent memory. Inter-state

strategic competition, not terrorism, is now the primary concern in U.S. national security.

China is a strategic competitor using predatory economics to intimidate its neighbors while militarizing features in the South China Sea. Russia has violated the borders of nearby nations and pursues veto power over the economic, diplomatic, and security decisions of its neighbors. As well, North Korea's outlaw actions and reckless rhetoric continue despite United Nation's censure and sanctions. Iran continues to sow violence and remains the most significant challenge to Middle East stability. Despite the defeat of ISIS's physical caliphate, threats to stability remain as terrorist groups with long reach continue to murder the innocent and threaten peace more broadly.[4]

According to the NSS, China and Russia are not just powerful counterparts, they are adversaries. In the National Defense Strategy, the term is "strategic competitor." In other contexts, such as Trump's 2018 State of the Union Address, they are "revisionist" powers. The NSS says of them the following:

China and Russia challenge American power, influence, and interests, attempting to erode American security and prosperity. They are determined to make economies less free and less fair, to grow their militaries, and to control information and data to repress their societies and expand their influence.[5]

Their goal, in other words, is not just to improve their own lot but to worsen America's. The National Defense Strategy goes even further:

It is increasingly clear that China and Russia want to shape a world consistent with their authoritarian model—gaining veto authority over other nations' economic, diplomatic, and security decisions . . . China and Russia are now undermining the international order from within the system by exploiting its benefits while simultaneously undercutting its principles and "rules of the road."[6]

One of the motifs running through these documents is that the United States naïvely tried the cooperative approach, but that it failed because of the perfidious behavior of America's adversaries:

These competitions require the United States to rethink the policies of the past two decades—policies based on the assumption that engagement with rivals and their inclusion in international institutions and global commerce would turn them into benign actors and trustworthy partners. For the most part, this premise turned out to be false.

Rival actors use propaganda and other means to try to discredit democracy. They advance anti-Western views and spread false information to create divisions among ourselves, our allies, and our partners.[7]

The first thing that comes to my mind is Jesus's admonition: "Why do you see the speck that is in your brother's eye, but do not notice the log that is in your own eye?" The U.S. security state is pointing its finger at China and Russia as undermining the global system. Yet which country launched catastrophic wars of "regime change" without requisite UN backing and against the advice of countries around the world? Which country has failed to ratify a UN-backed treaty in nearly a quarter-century (as I'll look at in detail in chapter 15)? Which country is repeatedly taking foreign policy measures strongly repudiated by most other countries, whether Trump's announced withdrawal from the Paris Climate Agreement or the move of America's Israeli embassy from Tel Aviv to Jerusalem over the objections of the other fourteen UN Security Council members?

The NSS's bleak assessment regarding global cooperation is belied by the facts, except of course if the bleakness becomes a self-fulfilling prophecy. The entire world (including the Obama administration) agreed on the future direction of development cooperation by adopting Agenda 2030 and the seventeen Sustainable Development Goals in September 2015, and signing the Paris Climate Agreement in December 2015 just a few weeks later. Most countries of the world, including China and Russia, have signed and ratified several important UN treaties during the past quarter-century, many of which, unfortunately, have been repudiated not by China and Russia but by the United States. On the great questions of military security, including the nuclear arsenal, it is hard to argue that China and Russia have been the instigators of bad behavior. The United States was the first to undermine U.S.-Russian nuclear cooperation by unilaterally abandoning the Anti-Ballistic Missile (ABM) Treaty in 2002 in order to pursue America's missile defense deployment. The United States led the expansion of NATO to Russia's backyard.

Consistent with exceptionalism, the United States has insisted on military dominance, not merely deterrence, in all regions of the world. When the United States vastly outspends China and Russia in military armaments and those countries respond by increasing their own arms spending, the United States then points an accusing finger. I am reminded of the cartoon in which the little boy runs to his mother crying, "Mommy, mommy, Jimmy hit me back." The other countries are indeed pushing back against U.S. assertions of dominance. That does not make them systems breakers.

One of the reasons why the National Security Strategy regards cooperation so bleakly is that it largely rejects the very need for cooperation. Instead of looking for global cooperation to decarbonize the world's energy system in order to achieve the globally agreed climate goals, the document instead declares that "U.S. leadership is indispensable to countering an anti-growth energy agenda that is detrimental to U.S. economic and energy security interests." There is not even lip service paid to other environmental challenges such as deforestation, loss of biodiversity, and water scarcity. There is a passing mention, just one sentence, about disease control.

The National Security Strategy accuses China of undermining global cooperation. This is certainly not how China describes its role in the world. President Xi Jinping's speech to the Nineteenth Party Congress in October 2017 offered an important statement of China's viewpoint. Xi spoke of China's overarching goal of national rejuvenation following the disasters of imperialism, foreign invasion, civil war, and economic turmoil that gripped China in the nineteenth and twentieth centuries. He emphasized that China's goals depend on a peaceful and stable international environment:

> The dream of the Chinese people is closely connected with the dreams of the peoples of other countries; the Chinese Dream can be realized only in a peaceful international environment and under a stable international order. We must keep in mind both our internal and international imperatives, stay on the path of peaceful development, and continue to

pursue a mutually beneficial strategy of opening up. We will uphold justice while pursuing shared interests, and will foster new thinking on common, comprehensive, cooperative, and sustainable security. We will pursue open, innovative, and inclusive development that benefits everyone; boost cross-cultural exchanges characterized by harmony within diversity, inclusiveness, and mutual learning; and cultivate ecosystems based on respect for nature and green development. China will continue its efforts to safeguard world peace, contribute to global development, and uphold international order.[8]

He then went on to outline the principles that would guide China's foreign policy, declaring that China "will continue to hold high the banner of peace, development, cooperation, and mutual benefit and uphold its fundamental foreign policy goal of preserving world peace and promoting common development." In this context, Xi issued a call for global cooperation, rejecting balance-of-power politics:

We call on the peoples of all countries to work together to build a community with a shared future for mankind, to build an open, inclusive, clean, and beautiful world that enjoys lasting peace, universal security, and common prosperity. We should respect each other, discuss issues as equals, resolutely reject the Cold War mentality and power politics, and take a new approach to developing state-to-state relations with communication, not confrontation and partnership, not alliance. We should commit to settling disputes through dialogue and resolving differences through discussion, coordinate responses to traditional and non-traditional threats and oppose terrorism in all its forms.[9]

Xi cites One Belt, One Road, China's development assistance, and China's support for the United Nations as specific ways that China is "ready to work with the people of all other countries to build a community with a shared future for mankind."

While many countries have serious concerns about China's rising power and how it will be used, Trump's naked assertion of America First has dramatically altered global perceptions of U.S. leadership. According to an early 2018 Gallup report on public approval of the leadership of Germany, the United States, China, and Russia, global confidence in U.S. leadership plummeted from 48 percent in 2016, the final year of the Obama administration, to just 30 percent in 2017.[10] Global public approval of China's leadership held steady at 31 percent. A mid-2017 Pew survey found the same, with confidence in Xi Jinping at 28 percent compared with just 22 percent for Trump.[11] If nothing else, America First has set off alarm bells around the world.

The National Security Strategy and National Defense Strategy are based squarely on the central pillar of American exceptionalism: global military dominance. The National Defense Strategy puts it this way: "For decades the United States has enjoyed uncontested or dominant superiority in every operating domain. We could generally deploy our forces when we wanted, assemble them where we wanted, and operate how we wanted. Today, every domain is contested—air, land, sea, space, and cyberspace." The stated goal is to "remain the preeminent military power in the world," and in particular to maintain "favorable regional balances of power in the Indo-Pacific, Europe, the Middle East, and the Western Hemisphere."[12]

To sustain its military dominance, the United States maintains a costly network of nearly 800 military bases in more than seventy countries around the world, at an estimated annual cost of around $100 billion as of 2014, according to author David Vine.[13] (China, as I've mentioned, has only one small overseas base, in Djibouti.) Vine's global map of overseas U.S. military facilities, shown in figure 9.1, distinguishes between full bases, smaller "lily pads" with fewer than 200 personnel, and suspected but unconfirmed facilities.

The logic (or illogic) of "dominance" compels the U.S. military to keep expanding its geographic presence. NATO expanded eastward even after the Soviet threat disappeared. And after the United States ostensibly ended its combat missions in Afghanistan and Iraq, military bases and personnel remained behind. Most recently, the United States

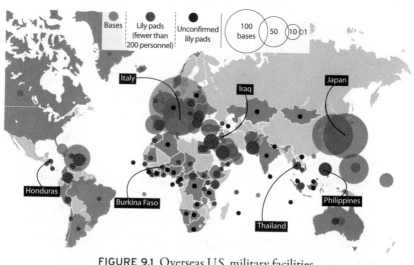

FIGURE 9.1 Overseas U.S. military facilities

Source: David Vine, "Where in the World Is the U.S. Military?" *Politico Magazine*, July/August 2015, https://www.politico.com/magazine/story/2015/06/us-military-bases-around-the-world-119321.

has announced its intention to create a base in Syria as well. Of course, nobody asked the Syrians their view on this. After all, the United States has remained in Guantanamo Bay Naval Base, Cuba, for 115 years despite ardent Cuban protests from the start.

The next big military price tag will be the upgrading of America's nuclear triad (land, air, and submarine). All signatories to the Nuclear Non-Proliferation Treaty, including the United States, are obligated under Article VI to "pursue negotiations in good faith on effective measures relating to cessation of the nuclear arms race at an early date and to nuclear disarmament, and on a treaty on general and complete disarmament under strict and effective international control."[14] Yet this has become a dead letter from the point of view of U.S. foreign policy. The new Nuclear Posture Review states, "We must look reality in the eye and see the world as it is, not as we wish it to be."[15] So much for treaty obligations. The Nuclear Posture Review calls for modernizing U.S. nuclear forces at a cost of around $1 trillion over the coming thirty years.

The U.S. strategy of military dominance will ultimately prove too costly to sustain now that China is ready to invest heavily to narrow the military gap with the United States. The Chinese believe they must make increased military investments to offset U.S. power, while the United States regards China's attempt to narrow the military gap with the United States as a dangerous provocation. The security dilemma rears its head once again. If the United States persists in trying to maintain military dominance, we will set off an enormous arms race with China, this time with a country that is four times larger by population and 20 percent larger by outputs than the United States (when GDP is measured at international prices per the IMF).

The United States is hastening the day of budgetary reckoning by expanding military spending while also cutting taxes, thereby increasing an already large budget deficit, now estimated to average 4–5 percent of GDP per year during the coming decade. All told, U.S. military spending currently amounts to around 5 percent of GDP if we add together the Pentagon, homeland security, nuclear weapons, the CIA and other intelligence agencies, and the costs of veterans' medical care and other benefits. With federal tax revenues running to only around 17 percent of GDP, the federal budget cannot even now cover the sum of military spending, interest on the debt, and big-ticket social programs such as Social Security and health care, much less the civilian discretionary programs such as job training, education, community development, environmental protection, and civilian research and development. These discretionary programs have already been cut to the bone, thereby weakening the economic foundations of American power.

Moreover, America's military predominance is already waning. In 1993, the United States accounted for 49 percent of the military outlays of the twenty largest military spenders.[16] By 2016, the U.S. share had declined to 43 percent. In practical terms, the decline is even larger. If we group the countries according to whether they are military allies of the United States, the decline in military outlays of the United States plus allies is much starker. In 1993, the United States plus its allies accounted for a whopping 94 percent of military outlays of the top-twenty spenders. By 2016, their share of military outlays had declined to 72 percent.[17]

The biggest shift was China, which accounted for 2 percent of the military outlays in 1993 but 15 percent in 2016. Russia went from 1 percent of top-twenty military outlays to 5 percent, while Iran went from 0.2 percent to 0.9 percent. It's no wonder that the United States regards China, Iran, and Russia as its main strategic competitors. Their rising military outlays, combined with their geopolitical independence, especially threaten America's military dominance.

One might argue that the United States will keep its military predominance by winning new allies (such as India) and by pushing existing allies to spend more on the military. The United States is of course trying both approaches. In my view, they will have limited effect. India, Pakistan, Russia, and other large economies have their own interests that they will not subordinate for the long term to those of the United States. They may be tactical allies on particular occasions, but in the long term they will pursue their own interests. The same is true of Turkey today, which is a U.S. ally under NATO but a competitor and part-time adversary in the Middle East.

Some will also predict that the United States will keep its predominance through its technological edge, but that too is a dubious proposition. China's capacity for innovation is soaring, as measured, for example, by the rapid increase in Chinese patents, R&D outlays, scientific publications, and shares of production and sales of commercial technologies. The same will occur with Russia, India, and other countries that are outside of the U.S. alliance. Sadly, one of the ways that America is maintaining high military spending is through cuts in outlays on science and technology. We'll look at the costs of such shortsighted decisions in the next part.

Part III

U.S. FOREIGN ECONOMIC STATECRAFT

The American economy has shown a mixed performance over the past quarter-century since the end of the Cold War. On the one hand, economic growth has continued, albeit at a rate that was less than the preceding quarter-century (roughly the 1960s through the 1980s). On the other hand, economic inequality soared, jobs were shed in manufacturing, and America divided into two economies—a prosperous one for those with four-year college degrees or more and a stagnant or declining economy for those with less education. I have described this divided economy in two recent books, *The Price of Civilization* (2012)[1] and *Building the New American Economy* (2017).[2]

Trump's America First policy is partly about economic statecraft. It is based on Trump's belief that the United States has been duped by its trading counterparts, such as China, Germany, and Mexico. Trump's misunderstanding is primitive, as he interprets America's trade deficit with these countries as proof that these countries are subjecting the United States to unfair trade practices. In fact, the U.S. trade deficit is a sign of America's extraordinarily low saving rate, which is itself partly due to excessive military spending and tax cuts that have boosted the federal budget deficit and led to negative rates of government saving.

Trump's economic policies are like his personality, impulsive and shortsighted, and likely to damage the working-class constituency he professes to support. Trump's fiscal policies will cause a soaring budget deficit that will eventually weaken America's fiscal standing and undermine the government's ability to invest in the future, including vital investments in science and technology. Trump's trade policies will not bring home millions of manufacturing jobs and might instead cause a trade war in which the United States itself will be among the losers. China's economic statecraft, on the other hand, based on regional integration (One Belt, One Road) and large, long-term investments in cutting-edge technologies, is very likely to boost China's global competitiveness as well as its environmental sustainability.

Trump's protectionism plays to his political base: white, less-educated workers who have lost jobs or wages as the result of globalization. But protectionism is the wrong way to address the real needs of such workers. Much better would be a combination of new job training, expanded wage subsidies through the Earned Income Tax Credit, and other forms of redistribution from the rich to the poor. As I have recently discussed those better alternatives elsewhere,[3] I will not repeat the arguments here.

Trump's nationalism is very poorly timed, as the world needs more global and regional cooperation, not less. The major problems that afflict us—global warming and other environmental threats, the need to upgrade energy infrastructure, rapid shifts in the labor market resulting from artificial intelligence and robotics—argue for solutions that require global and regional cooperation and policies that cannot be implemented by any one country alone, even the United States with its vast economy.

10

THE ECONOMIC BALANCE SHEET
ON "AMERICA FIRST"

President Donald Trump believes an "America First" foreign economic policy would save Americans' income
and jobs and would help rebuild the country. For
Trump, the economic content of America First is aggressive
trade protectionism, a closure of borders to migration, economic sanctions against U.S. adversaries, rejection of China's
investments in U.S. companies, and other measures to give the
United States a purported advantage in economic power vis-
à-vis America's rivals. Putting aside the moral and diplomatic
dangers in Trump's brazen assertion of American self-interest
above global well-being, there are several dangerous myths in
Trump's economic reasoning.

Trump's most provocative and misguided claims arise in
regard to America's international trade and investment policies.
He has repeatedly claimed that by getting tough with American
firms moving overseas to China and Mexico he will restore
American jobs and wealth at home. In this case, Trump has spot-
ted a true phenomenon—the offshoring of jobs—but grossly
exaggerated its importance and shot utterly at the wrong target.

American manufacturing companies have indeed moved
jobs to China and Mexico in order to benefit from lower wages

for the labor-intensive segments of the production process. A recent study shows that as of 2014, U.S. multinational firms employed around 706,000 manufacturing workers in Mexico and 753,000 in China, or about 1.5 million workers in total, in overseas affiliates in which the U.S. firms have majority ownership.[4] The Mexican production is directed toward the U.S. market under NAFTA, while the Chinese production is for both the United States and the rest of the world.

Of course, 1.5 million is not a trivial number of workers, but it amounts to just 1 percent of the U.S. labor force. Manufacturing jobs as a whole in the United States are just not that numerous anymore because of the long-term processes of automation. In 1970, manufacturing jobs constituted 25 percent of the workforce; today, they constitute just 8.4 percent. It's not that the manufacturing jobs went overseas; they mostly went the way of smart machines. Yesteryear's assembly workers are today's assembly-line robots. And today's remaining manufacturing workers are tomorrow's artificial intelligence systems.

There is another fallacy. Reversing the offshoring would not create the same 1.5 million jobs inside the United States. Production is much more capital intensive in the United States than in China and Mexico because of higher U.S. wages. The 1.5 million workers in China and Mexico might translate into 750,000 workers inside the United States. This is just 0.5 percent of the U.S. labor market. And even those supposed job gains overlook the much higher production costs that the U.S.-based companies would incur when the jobs return, causing those firms to lose international competitiveness and to cut back on other employment already in the United States, such as the R&D units that support overseas operations.

Of course, some offshore production will never return to the United States. Some of the overseas operations have nothing to do with the U.S. market. And even production for export to the U.S. market is not so easy to cajole back home.

Suppose, for example, that Trump were to follow through on his threat of a "border tax" (or import duty) on goods exported to the United States by U.S. companies operating in China and Mexico. In response, those companies would most likely divest their overseas operations and buy the same products from unaffiliated companies not subject to the border tax. Suppose that Trump were to put tariffs on products coming in from China and Mexico. He would then set off a gigantic trade war that would do great damage to the U.S. and world economy. This trade war may have started in slow motion in early 2018 with Trump's decision to impose protective tariffs on washing machines and solar panels (January) and steel and aluminum (March). The administration is also aggressively closing the U.S. market to China's high-tech companies such as Huawei on the grounds of national security.

What about pronouncements by Ford Motor Company, for example, promising to invest $700 million in Michigan rather than Mexico? The company declared that the move, portrayed as a response to Trump, would save 700 jobs, or roughly 1 job per $1 million in investments. At that rate, Trump is not going to get very far for America's 152 million workers. Indeed, as of January 2018, one year into the Trump program, U.S. employment in motor vehicles and parts manufacturing stood at 955,100, down from 956,700 in January 2017.

Instead of blaming China and Mexico for the very real problems facing America's workers, Trump should be taxing the booming incomes of the capital owners (with their stock valuations at record levels) in order to ease the economic burdens on the workers. Unfortunately, he is doing exactly the opposite: giving yet more tax breaks to corporate capital on the claim that corporate tax cuts will also bring manufacturing jobs back home.

The so-called tax "reform" of December 2017 is actually a tax monstrosity. It cuts the headline corporate tax rate from 35 percent to 21 percent with an estimated revenue loss of around $1.5 trillion over a decade, or roughly $150 billion per year. The estimated direct revenue loss plus higher interest payments on the public debt are likely to raise the overall budget deficit by nearly 1 percent of GDP per year during the decade 2018–2027, with the tax savings accruing overwhelmingly to the rich. Today's young people will inherit a mountain of public debt and debt servicing in the future. The debt/GDP ratio could rise from today's high ratio of 77 percent to nearly 100 percent by around 2030.

The gains in good new jobs will be very small. Indeed, much of the new investment by business will be in robotics and smart systems to *replace* workers, not to hire them. The tax cut could easily accelerate the shift away from labor toward capital in many sectors, thereby depressing real wages. Moreover, other nations will now cut their own corporate tax rates to prevent the United States from shifting investments out of those other economies. This will produce a "race to the bottom" in capital taxation. As more and more countries slash their corporate tax rates, no country gets an advantage over the others. Instead, they all lose revenues. The only winners are the richest people in the world, and even there, the "winning" is likely to be short-lived if the result is more political instability and social unrest.

Trump also proposes to offset the tax losses by slashing U.S. spending on foreign aid and on the United Nations. Here lies another great myth. Cutting spending on aid and the UN will save very little in dollar terms, but will cause a huge blow to

America's global interests and national security, not to mention America's moral standing in the world. Total U.S. foreign aid is around $33.6 billion per year, roughly 0.18 percent of national income. Thus, even if all foreign aid were eliminated, it would offset around one-fifth of Trump's corporate tax cut. If anything, the United States should be doing far more, in partnership with other countries; in chapter 16, I'll look at the important things U.S. foreign aid has accomplished—and all that could be accomplished with just a part of the funds that will go to the tax cuts for the rich.

Trump also asserts that the United States can achieve great savings by cutting its UN contributions. Here too, the savings are tiny in dollars and recklessly dangerous in their consequences. The United States contributes 22 percent of the UN's regular budget, the largest share of any country. But the regular budget is very modest, just $5.68 billion for the recent two years 2016–2017, with America's assessed share 22 percent of that, or just $625 million per year. Trump pushed for $285 million in cuts for the next two-year UN budget (2018–2019). The savings are thus $143 million per year, with the U.S. portion at 22 percent of that, or $31 million per year. That comes out to around 0.02 percent of the annual $150 billion in tax cuts.

The United States spends another $7 billion or so per year in so-called "voluntary contributions" for UN agencies such as UNICEF (the UN Children's Fund) and for UN peacekeeping operations. Not only are those additional contributions vital for saving lives and for U.S. and global security, but they are actually cost-saving for the United States as well. In each of these cases, the United States pools its funds with those of many other countries and thereby shares the global burden for peacekeeping, disease control, and other priorities. Many of those other donor countries give a much higher share of their GDP in aid and UN support than does the United States.

The main point is this: Even if all U.S. foreign aid and UN contributions were ended, the financial saving to the United States would amount to no more than 0.2 percent of GDP, roughly a quarter or a fifth of the 2017 tax cut, and roughly one-hundredth of the federal government's outlays. The idea that such savings would substantially benefit the American worker or taxpayer is a complete myth, indeed an outright hoax. The result of such budget cutting would be to make the world even more dangerous and unstable and more vulnerable to epidemic diseases and other natural disasters.

The bottom line is that "America First" will not solve America's jobs crisis, income inequality, or infrastructure crisis. American companies will bring few if any jobs back from China and Mexico. Slashing U.S. development assistance or outlays for the UN will produce negligible budget savings at a high cost to U.S. global interests. The tax cut will cause a significant rise in the budget deficit with little effect on growth and employment.

The key to resolving America's ills depends on greater fairness, decency, and honesty within our own borders, and depends notably on how we share the benefits of advanced technologies such as robotics and artificial intelligence and the booming profits they are producing. The real counterpart of falling American working-class incomes is not the rise of Mexican or Chinese incomes but the soaring profits and incomes now going to the richest 1 percent of Americans. The key solutions for American workers lie right here at home, not in overseas military adventures, new arms races, or self-defeating trade wars. Yet given Trump's misguided economic populism, that's exactly where we're headed.

11

FOREIGN POLICY POPULISM

L isten to President Trump describe how he will make America great again. He will deport illegal migrants, slash corporate taxes, build a wall, and make Mexico pay. He will punish companies that move jobs abroad, stand up to China's trade juggernaut, deregulate the economy, and end environmental protection.

The ostensible motivation for all this is faster economic growth and more jobs for working-class Americans. Properly viewed, economic growth and decent jobs are long-term challenges requiring a long-term national strategy. The nation's output depends on the productive assets in the economy, defined broadly to include the skills, technological know-how, roads, ports, factories, clean air and water, and even the trust in society that underpin commerce and finance. Economists call these assets the "capital" of the economy, including human capital (education, job skills, health); infrastructure capital (roads, power, fiber, rail); natural capital (clean air and water, fertile soils, robust biodiversity, a stable climate); intellectual capital (scientific and technological know-how); and social capital (trust among Americans). Long-term improvements in the economy depend on investing in the capital stock in these areas in a balanced and thoughtful way.

With the ongoing brilliant advances in technology, improved ways to impart skills to young people, smart infrastructure such as intercity fast rail and self-driving vehicles, environmental safety through the mass deployment of renewable energy, and a fairer income distribution to rebuild social trust, the American economy could indeed make substantial progress and raise future well-being.

A key policy step would be to boost national saving by increasing taxes on capital income, carbon emissions, and consumption spending in order to boost public-sector saving and investment in infrastructure, skills, and technology. (Barack Obama talked about this approach but didn't implement it. He never presented a plan or budget along these lines, even in the early days when he had Democratic majorities in both houses of Congress.)

This is the opposite of Trump's approach. Trump lives in a world of shortcuts: raising national income not by innovation, skill, and saving, but by grabbing income from somewhere else, such as Mexico, China, the environment, or future generations. Trump is the quintessential impulsive populist. History teaches why such short-termism is doomed to fail.

Almost thirty years ago, while working to end hyperinflation in Latin America, I made a study of Latin American short-termism. I tracked how short-term promises often ended up as long-term disasters in what I termed the "populist cycle," something like the business cycle but politically caused. In the case of Latin American populists, such as Argentina's Juan Perón and Venezuela's Hugo Chavez, their trick was to grab the government's financial assets and cash flow and, rather than invest them in the future, to distribute them among their followers in cash benefits, higher wages, and expanded public services.

Some of these short-term benefits can be real. The problem is paying for them in the long term. Over time, the public sector loses its cash reserves and builds up debt. Eventually the debt comes due and no new creditors are ready to lend the government more funds. When the creditors demand repayment, there are no funds available. The government starts printing money, inflation soars, and the debt is defaulted.

Post-Chavez Venezuela is essentially in that condition today. The government can't pay its bills. Inflation is soaring, and foreign exchange is so scarce that Venezuela can't afford to import food from abroad. Hunger is soaring, and children are dying. Such is the extreme populist cycle of boom followed by bust.

Trump is looking for short-term miracles to give quick gratification to his followers and carry him to reelection in 2020. Like Perón and Chavez, he'll try to grab what he can, both from foreigners and from future generations. He wants to crow about short-term gains. The question is how far he'll get and what mess he will leave behind.

He isn't getting very far with Mexico. His demand that Mexico build and pay for a border wall was met with an emphatic no. Then came the suggestion that Trump would slap on a tariff to pay for it, as part of corporate tax reforms. Many businesses operating in Canada and Mexico expressed strong opposition to such a border tax and killed the proposal. Meanwhile, Trump pressures American companies to invest in the United States rather than in Mexico, another kind of grab from Mexico, but aside from winning some headlines, it's hard to believe that the results will reach any meaningful scale in U.S. jobs created.

The attempt to grab benefits from China looks to be even less successful. The administration arrived in office boasting of the coming trade wars with China. Trump wants to wrong-foot China through multiple pressures on trade, foreign policy, and defense, and then negotiate some kind of winning trade deal to America's advantage. Yet China's President Xi Jinping has made clear that if the United States turns protectionist, China will continue to lead in free trade. And if the United States cuts its support for multilateralism at the UN and elsewhere, China will be pleased to help support the multilateral order. It won't be so easy, after all, to bully China. China's economy is now larger than America's. China is a major consumer of American goods that could easily be sourced elsewhere (buy Airbus rather than Boeing). And China is America's creditor, holding hundreds of billions of dollars of U.S. financial assets and helping to finance America's chronic budget deficits.

Trump's grab for short-term income does not end with Mexico and China. The tax cuts enacted in December 2017 are similarly conceived. The tax cuts aim to shift investments from the rest of the world to the U.S. economy, cutting investments and jobs abroad while boosting them in the United States. Yet there are three fundamental limitations to this approach.

First, America's overtaxation was greatly exaggerated in the lead-up to the tax cut. Many detailed provisions of the pre-2018 tax code (such as accelerated depreciation, deductions for U.S.-based production, expensing of R&D, and the deductibility of interest payments on corporate debt) lowered the effective marginal tax rate on capital below the "headline" rate of 35 percent. As a result, cutting the headline corporate tax rate from 35 to 21 percent will have a much smaller effect on investment incentives than was claimed in the tax cut debate, since the incentives for investment before the tax cuts were already reasonably strong.

Second, other countries will certainly respond to the U.S. corporate tax cuts with a new round of cuts of their own. As mentioned earlier, we are in a global "race to the bottom" in corporate taxation, as each country cuts its corporate tax rate to entice internationally mobile companies to the home shores. As a result, all of the competing countries could end up with near-zero corporate tax rates, unless we are wise enough to cooperate with other countries to stop this race to the bottom.

Third, the loss of corporate tax revenues will need to be paid for somehow, a point that populists like Trump and the Republican tax cutters in Congress have tried to evade. Trump's hidden reasoning might be simple: he doesn't pay taxes, so why should anybody else? Trump will not offset the proposed tax cuts with spending cuts, such as on the military; indeed, he has proposed spending increases on infrastructure and the military.

The Trump and Republican plan is to finance the tax cuts mainly by increased budget deficits. That's a hidden way of making today's young people pay for tax cuts on behalf of old and rich capitalists. It is the young—the millennials— who will pay higher taxes during their lifetimes to service the mountain of public debt that Trump will leave behind. If Trump won't be able to grab income so easily from Mexico, from China, and from other competitor nations, will he get away with grabbing wealth from today's young people? This is probably the central question that Republicans will soon confront at the polls.

Trump has spied one more place to grab some income in the short term, and that is from natural capital, the environment.

Trump's first new infrastructure projects, he hopes, will be oil and gas pipelines to boost fossil-fuel production, despite the consequences of more global warming. By ruining the climate and despoiling the air and water, Trump aims to grab one more round of profits for his friends in the coal, oil, and gas sectors. He does this in the name of the mining and oil-rig workers, but their employment is already small and falling, as these jobs are increasingly replaced by automation.

Trump's antienvironmental populism—destroying the Earth for a trickle of profits today—is perhaps the most insidious and irreversible of all of his populist ploys. Mexico can answer back; China can put its foot down; other countries can plan to match the United States in tax cuts. But who will speak up for the Earth? Who will speak up for our children and grandchildren, who will inherit a degraded planet if Trump gets his way? That will have to be the job for all of us.

An overriding element of economic confusion pervades Trump's America First agenda, and that involves the U.S. trade deficit. Trump and his commerce secretary Wilbur Ross claim that America's trade deficit is an indicator of unfair trade practices by foreign countries, especially Germany and China, two trade surplus countries. Their embrace of this mistaken idea could lead to disaster.

Here is the basic idea: When a country saves some of its current output, it can use that output for investments. But what if the nation's saving is larger than its investments? Then the nation can export the remaining output. If the nation's saving is greater than its investment, there is output left over for exports. If the nation's saving is less than its investment, it will have to import goods from abroad to carry out the investments.

We can see intuitively that when the nation's saving exceeds its investment spending, the country runs a trade surplus (exports larger than imports), and when the saving is less than the investment spending, the country runs a trade deficit (imports larger than exports). This statement requires some technical refinements, especially to take into account the earnings by Americans on overseas assets such as foreign businesses, and the payments to foreigners on the assets they own in the United States. The correct technical statement is that a country's current account balance, which is closely related to the trade balance, is equal to the nation's saving minus its domestic investment.

The United States imports more from abroad than it exports because the U.S. saving rate is chronically lower than the U.S. domestic investment rate. If Americans saved more, the United States would export more. For 2016, according to the IMF World Economic Outlook database, the U.S. saving rate was 18 percent of GDP, compared with the German saving rate of 27.5 percent and China's saving rate of 45.9 percent. U.S. saving was not enough to cover the U.S. investment rate at 19.7 percent of GDP, while in both Germany and China, the domestic saving rate was greater than the investment rate, leaving a surplus for export.

Trump, with exquisite economic illiteracy, has missed this whole point. For Trump, the fact that China and Germany export more than they import has only to do with China's and Germany's unfair trade practices. With his conspiratorial mind-set, Trump believes that America's trade deficit simply means that somebody is taking advantage of the United States. He is, in fact, both economically illiterate and famously paranoid, always supposing a conspiracy someplace.

The real question, one that Trump and his administration have not asked is, why the U.S. saving rate is so low? Why do China and Germany save so much more of their national income than the United States? Why has the U.S. saving rate declined markedly over the past forty years, notably after 1980, thereby causing the U.S. current account balance to shift from a surplus to a deficit? One key reason is that the federal government itself stopped saving. Starting in the 1980s, the federal government repeatedly enacted tax cuts, pushing the government into deficit. With the government spending more than its income, the nation's saving—which equals the sum of private saving and government saving—declined overall.

Here we see that Trump's economic illiteracy will come back to bite the United States twice. The new round of tax cuts will widen the budget deficit and also widen the trade deficit (because of the fall in national saving). As the trade deficit widens, Trump is likely to pursue even more protection-ist policies, accusing America's trade partners of unfair trade practices, when it is Trump's own tax-cutting policies that have pushed the United States even deeper into the red. Trump is likely to "retaliate" with higher tariffs and more protectionism against alleged unfair practices abroad that have nothing to do with their actual trade policies. Rarely has economic policy, in this case U.S. trade policy, been built on such folly.

Ideas matter—in this case, very bad ideas. The emperor has no clothes and, it seems, no competent economic advisers either.

12

ECONOMIC WAR WITH CHINA

Today's China offers a rude awakening for Americans who believe that the United States and the United States alone should be the dominant world power. Donald Trump seems to count himself among these neoconservatives, and China is their deepest phobia today. Trump is following a game plan that has characterized U.S. "grand strategy" against major rivals dating back to World War II. Each time America has had a rival for global leadership, the United States has aimed to cut the rival down to size and to subordinate it to U.S. power. For a while it worked, at least to a point.

In the 1970s, the United States briefly faced what it believed to be another major rival for economic power, Japan. Japan's post–World War II recovery was so dynamic, and its mastery of the new transistor-based electronics so strong in the 1960s, that many business and economic gurus in the 1970s envisioned a future world economy dominated by Japanese companies and wealth. I remember studies in the early 1980s that naïvely extrapolated Japan's rapid growth and high saving rates forward for several decades to argue that the United States would be the sure loser in the long-run competition with Japan.

Starting with President Ronald Reagan, the U.S. foreign policy establishment went to work to counter Japan. It began accusing Japan of unfair trade practices, currency manipulation, unfair state aid to Japan's businesses, and other exaggerated or flat-out false claims of nefarious behavior. The United States began to impose new trade barriers and forced Japan to agree to "voluntary" export restraints to limit its booming exports to the United States. Then, in 1985, the United States struck harder, insisting that Japan massively revalue (strengthen) the yen in a manner that would leave Japan far less competitive with the United States. The yen doubled in value, from 260 yen per dollar in 1985 to 130 yen per dollar in 1990. The United States had pushed Japan to price itself out of the world market. By the early 1990s, Japan's export growth collapsed, and Japan entered two decades of stagnation. On many occasions after 1990, I asked senior Japanese officials why Japan didn't devalue the yen to restart growth. The most convincing answer was that the United States wouldn't let Japan do it.

Now comes China. American exceptionalists are beside themselves that China seems to have the audacity to poke its nose into the American Century. And China is doing this as a surprise entrant to the race, at least a surprise from a twentieth-century perspective, making its recent rise even more unnerving to exceptionalists. According to estimates from the IMF World Economic Outlook database, China's total output is now 24 percent larger than America's, and China's output per person is around 29 percent of America's, all measured at international prices.

Many American exceptionalists can't believe their eyes. Some argue that China's economy is a giant bubble that will soon implode, following the way of the Soviet Union. This is not the case in my view. The Soviet economy was technologically separated from the U.S.-led trading system and, in the end, could not keep up. China, by contrast, has achieved its remarkable economic growth since 1980 precisely by adopting global technologies and integrating the Chinese economy closely with the world economy. More recently, China has become a highly innovative economy as well, spreading cutting-edge technologies to other parts of the world.

Rather than let China catch up, the exceptionalists say, the United States should badger and harass China economically, engage the Chinese in a new arms race, and even undermine the One China policy that has been the basis of U.S.-China bilateral relations, so that China ends up in economic retreat, retracing the steps of the British Empire, the Soviet Union, and Japan. One theory making the rounds indeed holds that Trump wants to sidle up to Vladimir Putin to team up against China for just this purpose.

In my view, such an approach toward China would be profoundly misguided and very dangerous. It is based on the false idea that global economics must be about winners versus losers, the United States versus China, rather than about mutual gains through trade and technological advance. Moreover, the idea of cornering China is not only unwise but unachievable.

Trump blames China for the plight of American workers left unemployed by China's exports to the United States, but he fails to understand or acknowledge the many gains to the United States from our trade with China, including the higher profits and wages of U.S. companies exporting to China and the lower costs enjoyed by U.S. consumers of China's exports. If Trump really wants to help American workers, he should tax and redistribute the soaring U.S. profits and incomes of the rich, rather than open a trade war with China.

Even worse, an American effort to weaken China is doomed to fail. When the United States pressed Britain to give up its empire, Britain was fighting for its very survival, and with a population just one-third that of the United States. When the United States pressured Japan in the 1980s, Japan's economy was only one-third of America's, and Japan depended on the United States for its military security.

China, by contrast, has a larger economy, is four times more populous, and is America's creditor, not its debtor. China has strong and growing trade, investment, and diplomatic relations with other countries all over the world that would likely be strengthened, not weakened, by U.S. belligerence. It's also important to remember that China's proud history as a unified nation is ten times longer than America's, around 2,250 years compared with around 225 years.

Aside from the usual litany of exaggerated or false charges against China (currency manipulator, unfair trader, etc.), the most recent rap is that China is a dangerously expansionist power. If ever the pot has called the kettle black, here is a case. I have already mentioned the wild divergence in foreign military bases (China has one overseas base, the United States has bases in seventy countries) and that the United States outspends China on the military by more than two to one. Consider as well that while the United States has been in nonstop overseas wars and regime-change operations for decades, China has been in very few overseas conflicts, all short-lived. While there's room to be concerned about China's territorial claims in the South China Sea, so far those maritime claims seem mainly designed to secure China's trade routes rather than to impede the neighboring countries.

In short, China has not been an expansionist or aggressive power in recent decades, while the United States has sought the unrivaled dominance of global military power with a network of hundreds of military bases around the world.

While the United States cannot dominate China, it need not fear China's dominance either. Yes, China is now larger economically than the United States, and will remain so, but the United States remains far richer in per capita terms and will likely continue to be so throughout the twenty-first century. Moreover, China's high growth rates are now slowing markedly, not because the Chinese economy is collapsing but because it is maturing. "Catching-up" growth slows down as it succeeds. Also, China is aging rapidly and will have a median age above fifty years by midcentury, along with a gradually declining population. A mature, aging, and slower-growing economy that is still much poorer than the United States in per capita terms is hardly a deep threat to America's own security or global security.

If Trump tries to provoke China into a new arms race or trade war, the results will be a huge debacle for the United States and a potential threat for the world. America's well-being depends on the maturity of judgment to cooperate with China as a major global power that can and should share the responsibilities of promoting global peace and sustainable development. Working through the United Nations, China and the United States can and should work together and with other countries to prevent or end regional wars, stop terrorism, and confront common hazards such as global warming and newly emerging diseases.

The United States would be wise not just to cooperate with China, but also to emulate its recent increased investments in science and technology. While not conductive to the short-term populism of Trump's America First policies, technological strength is the key to long-term growth, as I discuss in the next chapter.

13

WILL TRUMP HAND CHINA THE TECHNOLOGICAL LEAD?

President Trump is putting America's capacity to innovate at the gravest risk in modern U.S. history. His proposals to cut federal support for scientific research are tantamount to passing the baton of global technology leadership to China, just as China is redoubling its own efforts to spur cutting-edge science. The losses from Trump's antiscience approach will be global, not America's alone. Scientists and engineers from the United States, the European Union, China, India, and other countries should be working together to find technical breakthroughs in areas such as low-carbon energy systems, infectious disease control, and global food security.

There are ample precedents of highly successful cross-country collaborative R&D in physics (e.g., CERN's discovery of the Higgs boson), genomics (the global collaboration to sequence the human and other genomes), astronomy and space science (the international space station), and Earth observation systems (for climate and pollution monitoring), among many areas. Such cooperation today would greatly enhance progress toward sustainable development and climate safety. Yet, the United States is moving in the opposite direction.

Sadly, Trump is playing out the game plan of the Republican far right, led by the Koch brothers, to cut taxes for the rich and then slash government spending, including R&D, to partially rebalance the budget. Yet the budget cutting comes in the midst of one of history's great technological revolutions. The remarkable advances in artificial intelligence, computer architecture, nanotechnology, genomics, neuroscience, and other fields are opening up new possibilities for zero-carbon energy, high-productivity agriculture, low-cost high-quality health care, lifelong online learning, personalized medicine, conservation biology, and other opportunities vital for sustainable development. Now is precisely the time to be increasing rather than cutting the government's backing for cutting-edge research and development.

In the first great phase of American industrialization, roughly from 1800 to 1950, America's industrial success was mostly a matter of an expanding domestic market. Key infrastructure, such as the Erie Canal in the first half of the nineteenth century and the transcontinental railway in the second half, created an enormous continental-scale market for industrial goods. The process included the good (inventors such as Samuel Morse, Thomas Edison, and Alexander Bell), the bad (considerable theft of European technologies), and of course the horrendously ugly (slavery and the genocide of Native Americans).

World War II marked a pivotal transition in the nature of United States—and indeed, of global—innovation. The physical sciences and advanced engineering became far more central to the entire innovation process. And government became far more essential to advances in science and engineering.

Starting in the 1930s, with the mass influx of world-leading European scientists fleeing Hitler, the United States became the new global capital of cutting-edge science and technology.

After World War II, the U.S. military recruited scientists from the defeated Nazi regime as well, such as rocket scientist Werner van Braun.

Equally important, World War II fundamentally changed how technological innovation was pursued. Throughout the war, the U.S. military worked closely with top scientists and private enterprises to develop new military technologies on a targeted and emergency basis. Countless areas of technology were radically advanced by directed efforts of government working with academia and industry.

This quintessential wartime innovation process came to be known as "directed technological change." The military and scientists would interactively identify new technological possibilities, and government would finance the requisite research and development. The most famous example is the Manhattan Project to develop the atomic bomb. There were many other lesser-known but momentous cases. And new materials developed for military technologies, such as semiconductor materials used for the new radar technology, became cornerstones of postwar industry. The breakthroughs in semiconductors, for example, became the basis for the invention of the transistor in 1947.

At the end of World War II, FDR's science adviser, Vannevar Bush, wrote the visionary manifesto of the new era of innovation, *Science: The Endless Frontier*. Bush brilliantly envisioned, and helped to create, a new era in which government, academia, and industry cocreated innovations based on advanced science and technology. Bush's vision was motivated first by national security—the belief that America's military predominance depended on American technological leadership—yet with the more general aim of promoting postwar American prosperity on the foundations of science-based industries.

The United States established a host of transformative institutions for science-based innovation, including the National Science Foundation (1950), the National Institutes of Health (1948), the Defense Advanced Research Project Agency (DARPA, 1958) of the Department of Defense, the Atomic Energy Commission (1946), the National Aeronautics and Space Administration (NASA, 1948), and others. Regulated monopolies such as Bell Telephone also maintained cutting-edge research laboratories that funded and supported fundamental advances in science and technology.

In countless areas of modern life, directed technological change became the guiding force of postwar progress. Government and civil-society organizations (such as the Rockefeller Foundation, in areas of public health and agriculture, and the March of Dimes, in the case of polio) would identify a cutting-edge opportunity. Scientific and engineering leaders in academia, national laboratories, and private industry would work together to chart possible pathways to success, and the government and foundations would fund the R&D and also support the subsequent diffusion of successful innovations. Thus, the March of Dimes, originally launched by President Roosevelt in 1938, funded Jonas Salk's breakthrough research that produced the first successful polio vaccine, and the government then funded the vaccine's rapid uptake.

In this way, government funding and leadership supported key advances in science and technology that could thereafter be scaled up by government and private industry. Successes included the moonshot, the rapid development of computer science, the invention of the Internet, advances in exploration and development of hydrocarbons (including hydraulic fracturing, or fracking), advances in crop breeding, the sequencing of the human genome, and more recently, self-driving vehicles championed by DARPA.

The close working relationship among government, academia, and business is the essence of directed technological change that has contributed in fundamental ways to America's technological edge, global competitiveness, rising living standards, and national security. Budgetary requirements are often enormous—billions of dollars for early-stage R&D. The resulting national innovation system is complex, with crucial interactions across key stakeholders (academia and business, for example) over the course of a decade or two.

Advances in science and technology are hard won. Most importantly, government must be the champion of scientific truth over politics and must be ready to invest for the long run. Alas, these foundations for long-term innovation have deteriorated badly in recent years, and the Trump administration constitutes a new, unimaginable low point.

Trump and his cronies have their eyes narrowly and obsessively fixed on two goals: deregulation and tax cuts, both of which work against long-term innovation. The relentless focus on tax cuts and deregulation is the libertarian agenda long championed by the far right. It now threatens to kill the federal innovation system, the one that Vannevar Bush helped to put in place nearly seventy-five years ago.

The result is a politics of lies and slashed budgets for federally funded R&D. Basic science—for example, the well-established science of climate change—is trashed in order to promote antiscientific environmental deregulation. And the budgets of the government's key scientific agencies and laboratories are slashed to facilitate further tax cuts for the rich. In the process, the Republican Party has firmly become an antiscience party.

It's striking how dramatically the situation has deteriorated, even when compared with the administration of George W. Bush, an administration that, like Trump's, was also dominated by the oil-and-gas lobby. While the Bush administration rejected any meaningful policies to combat climate change and parroted antiscience in the process, it did recognize the importance of science and technology for America's long-term competitiveness.

The administration and Congress backed an important 2005 study, *Rising Above the Gathering Storm*, by the National Academy of Sciences (NAS).[1] The report strongly endorsed federal funding of R&D, a welcoming environment for international researchers to work in the United States, and improved science and mathematics education at the K–12 level in order to prepare young Americans for advanced studies in the sciences and engineering.

The opening words of the NAS study were striking and remain true today:

The prosperity the United States enjoys today is due in no small part to investments the nation has made in research and development at universities, corporations, and national laboratories over the last 50 years. Recently, however, corporate, government, and national scientific and technical leaders have expressed concern that pressures on the science and technology enterprise could seriously erode this past success and jeopardize future US prosperity.

The commission made four key recommendations: "Increase America's talent pool by vastly improving K–12 science and mathematics education; sustain and strengthen the nation's traditional commitment to long-term basic research;

make the United States the most attractive setting in which to study and perform research; and ensure that the United States is the premier place in the world to innovate."

These recommendations were broadly adopted in the America Competes Act of 2007, which established important new initiatives for federally funded research and development and support for education in STEM (science, technology, engineering, and mathematics). The legislation created the extremely important Advanced Research Project Agency in the Department of Energy (ARPA-E) to support R&D on cutting-edge energy technologies.

Now Trump is dismantling or degrading virtually every piece of the civilian innovation system. First, Trump's first budget aimed to eliminate ARPA-E entirely and to slash federal outlays on biomedical research as well, cutting the annual budget for the National Institutes of Health from around $30 billion to $25 billion. The budget for the Department of Education was also sharply reduced, by around 13 percent, or $9 billion. While Congress, including many Republican members, resisted these proposed cuts, Trump continues to chip away at funding for civilian science and technology.

Second, Trump has begun shutting down the scientific capacity of U.S. agencies to deal with environmental science and environmental crises such as climate change and pollution. Federal websites have gone silent on climate science; online data sets that were once available to the scientific community are being withdrawn; agencies have been put on warning against discussing climate change; and Trump has pushed hard for drastic cuts to the budget, slashing the Environmental Protection Agency to the core, including its Office of Research and Development. All of this attack on federally supported R&D is gravely compounded by Trump's own antiscience rhetoric.

Third, Trump's travel bans and general hostility to international partnerships and cooperation is already putting a severe chill on global scientific cooperation. It is no accident that American universities have lined up against the travel bans and have been plaintiffs seeking to prevent their implementation.

What is so remarkable about all of this is that Trump is degrading America's innovation system just as China is taking remarkably bold steps to upgrade its own innovation system and its leadership in cutting-edge technologies. China's rate of patenting has soared in recent years, nearly catching up with the rate of U.S. patent applications, and is on a path to overtake the United States in the near future. China is now producing more science and engineering PhDs than the United States. Perhaps most striking is China's explicit commitment to technological advances in ten critical sectors in the coming decade, part of a newly announced "Made in China 2025" program, including advanced information technology, new energy (including electric) vehicles, low-carbon energy, and advanced medical sciences, among others. America is ceding the field to China in key future technologies.

With rapid technological breakthroughs underway in many parts of the world, the added benefits of global cooperation are even greater. More than ever, global networks of scientists working together, and supported by national governments, could build on each other's expertise, test new approaches, and dramatically shorten the time span from initial hypothesis to scientific discovery to technical applications and global dissemination. Such global cooperative efforts would not only provide shared gains for all participating countries, but also reduce distrust across the world. Scientists speak a truly global language, and their shared successes could help all the rest of us to do so as well.

14

TOWARD A WORLD ECONOMY
OF REGIONS

There are very strong reasons for neighboring nations to cooperate. Neighbors share rivers and watersheds and other national resources. Neighbors may spread diseases across borders, requiring joint efforts for disease surveillance and epidemic control. Neighbors can usefully collaborate in building trans-boundary road, rail, power, and fiber networks. Neighbors can enjoy mutual benefits of tourism, trade, and financial flows. And, of course, neighbors gain by avoiding violence across the common border.

Nonetheless, the Cold War often divided neighbors, rather than uniting them. One country would be in the U.S. camp and the next-door neighbor in the Soviet camp. When disputes between neighbors arose, one would look to one superpower and the other then gravitate to the other. One might offer a military base to the United States, prompting the neighbor to request security help from the Soviet camp. Since both superpowers believed that their Cold War competition extended to every region of the world, every cross-border dispute among smaller nations had the potential to turn into a new battleground of the wider Cold War.

Of course there were ample reasons for cross-border tensions even without the meddling of the superpowers. Next-door neighbors dispute where boundaries are drawn (perhaps as the result of wars long past). They may each be home to an ethnic group that straddles the border, or that uses one country to launch attacks on the neighboring country. The current boundaries might have been drawn by the European imperial powers in ways that create major headaches today. Yet all of these headaches are greatly exacerbated when the quarreling neighbors turn to the major powers for support in their local battles. Local conflicts suddenly become regional or global conflicts, and even proxy wars among the superpowers.

Consider the morass of Syria today. Syria itself is a mosaic of ethnicities across many Muslim and Christian denominations. Three major regional Muslim powers, Turkey, Saudi Arabia, and Iran, all compete for influence, while Israel worries especially about Iran's potential influence and ability to supply weapons through Syria to Hezbollah in Lebanon and Hamas in Gaza. All of these countries worry about the possibility that a rival power will gain ascendancy in Syria. Turkey worries also about the possibility of a semi-independent Kurdish enclave in Syria that could then support the Kurdish national movement within Turkey.

During the Cold War, the Syrian regime of Hafez al-Assad was a Soviet client state, putting the United States on alert against possible Soviet actions in the region carried out via Syria. After 1992, the United States looked for opportunities to weaken or overthrow the Assad regime, partly to push Russia from the scene and partly to resist Iranian influence. When Bashar al-Assad succeeded his father, the United States tried alternatively to woo the son or to overthrow him. It settled on the latter approach upon the eruption of the Arab

Spring in early 2011. The U.S. government teamed up with Saudi Arabia, Israel, and Turkey to overthrow Assad, using the CIA to channel arms, money, and advice, while the Syrian government looked to Russia and Iran to save it.

All over the world, such regional tensions reflected local histories combined with great-power politics and interventions. In northeast Asia, China, Russia, and North Korea have long faced off against the United States, Japan, and South Korea. In South Asia, the United States has traditionally sided with Pakistan in its diplomatic and military standoff with India, though U.S. interests have recently shifted toward India. In these cases and countless others, local powers have competed for advantage by recruiting global powers as allies. In turn, the global powers have often found it convenient to compete with other global powers through their local proxies.

Add in natural resources such as oil, and local conflicts quickly become even more chaotic and multifaceted. Great-power interventions in the Middle East have inevitably involved jockeying for lucrative oil concessions, or for rights of way on pipelines, ports, and shipping lanes. Woe be the country that discovers oil, gas, diamonds, gold, or other riches under the ground. It is likely to become a playground for international intrigue if not outright war.

From an economic point of view, conflicts between neighbors are generally devastating for both. Even when war is avoided, mere diplomatic chilliness between neighbors can drain both countries of economic dynamism. When neighbors are friendly, on the other hand, they can capture the significant benefits of cross-border trade and finance; economies of scale in network infrastructure (power transmission, connectivity, storage, and transport); delivery of public health services (epidemic surveillance and control); and ecosystem management (biodiversity conservation, pollution control, and fresh water management, among others).

Regional economic and political integration, as in the European Union, is the single most powerful strategy to reduce the risks of war and increase the prospects for economic development. Europe's history in the twentieth century proves the point. After World War I, two defunct multiethnic empires (Austria-Hungary and Ottoman) splintered into small successor states with mutual distrust and hostility. Moreover, trade among the larger powers (Britain, France, Germany, Italy) was impeded by tariffs, inconvertible currencies, international debts, and deep diplomatic conflicts engendered by the Treaty of Versailles. The prewar Europewide trading system was utterly shattered. Europe experienced twenty years of nonstop economic crisis, including the monetary instability of the 1920s and the Great Depression of the 1930s. This generation-long economic crisis, in turn, created the conditions for renewed war.

After World War II, Germany and France were determined to put an end to the cycle of devastating war and retribution that had gripped those two countries for the preceding seventy-five years. The countries of Western Europe were especially keen to remain united in order to resist the dangers arising from Stalin's Soviet system. Thus, the European leaders, strongly encouraged by the United States, charted a path of increasing economic and political integration, starting with the Coal and Steel Community that brought France and Germany together in the 1950s and then the Treaty of Rome in 1957 that created the European Economic Community, later the European Union (EU). Europe moved toward a free market for goods, and later toward a single market for goods, services, capital, and labor.

The Treaty of Rome ushered in a period of rapid and equitable European growth that lasted from the late 1950s to the 1970s, and the European single market under the Maastricht and Lisbon treaties gave further impulse to Europe's political integration and economic expansion from the 1990s to the present. During this period, until Trump's accession to power, the United States viewed Europe's unity as of great benefit not only to Europe but to the United States as well, strengthening the NATO alliance and boosting Europe as a strong and reliable trading partner. Now Trump often seems to believe that the EU's weakness would somehow be to America's advantage, a bizarre view from the U.S. perspective and wholly outside of the American consensus of many decades.

With all of the European Union's many serious challenges—including heightened tensions over refugees and migration, unequal development between the richer north and poorer south, high youth unemployment, chronic economic crisis in Greece, cumbersome decision making, and repeated flare-ups of the euro and eurozone—Europe's economic and political integration has been hugely successful in reducing intra-European conflicts and promoting regionwide economic development. The EU is therefore a crucial role model for other parts of the world.

While there is much talk about a return to nationalism, with Trump even threatening to undo the North American Free Trade Area (NAFTA), my prediction is that regional integration is still in the ascendancy, not decline. The European Union is not about to disappear, and Britain's experience under Brexit will be a salutary warning to others that might flirt with the idea of going it alone. Around the world, the goal should be to overcome traditional disputes among neighbors to create similar processes of economic and political integration.

In northeast Asia, China is currently viewed as a strategic competitor and potential adversary of neighbors Japan and South Korea, which turn to the United States for their national security. Yet economic integration among the three countries is deepening despite the political divisions. The logic of economic cooperation is strong. The three countries are technological powerhouses that would be even more powerful if they cooperated closely on industrial standards; research and development; higher education; joint ventures in high-tech areas such as renewable energy, robotics, pollution control, and genomics; and transboundary infrastructure (energy, transport, connectivity). My own guess is that the three will establish a closer political modus operandi in the coming years, with the United States squeezed out of its current central role in the region's security arrangements. The world will then better appreciate the region as a world-leading technological colossus.

South Asia is another region where economic and political integration could lead to a huge advance in regional security and prosperity. Since the partition of British India in 1947, India and Pakistan have gone their separate ways, bearing deep grudges and enmities that have repeatedly spilled over into open conflicts. There have been four major conflicts (1947 upon partition, 1965, 1971, and 1999) and countless smaller conflicts and terrorist attacks. There are many causes of the rivalry and enmity, including the heatedly contested fate of Kashmir (a mostly Muslim Himalayan state claimed by both India and Pakistan), Hindu-Muslim relations, regional politics, and superpower politics. Both countries are nuclear powers, so their ongoing conflict is one of the world's most dangerous.

Trade, travel, and financial flows between the two giant countries are minimal, meaning that South Asia is squandering important opportunities for economic growth, infrastructure development, and technological advance. The two countries have important shared stakes in managing the Himalayan river systems, hydroelectric power, and renewable energy. Shared infrastructure would enable both countries to boost commerce, telecommunications, and linkages with other countries in Asia. As with the divisions between China, Japan, and South Korea, the rift between India and Pakistan cries out for compromise and reconciliation.

Africa is another region in desperate need of much closer political, economic, and financial integration. When the European imperial powers carved up Africa in the 1880s, they created a mosaic of national boundaries that suited European rivalries but made little sense in terms of ethnicity, watersheds, riverways, land transport, seaports, ecosystems, biodiversity, and mineral wealth. As a result of these arbitrary boundaries and their further division at the time of independence, Africa ended up with the largest number of landlocked nations of any major world region, fourteen of the fifty-four countries. Landlocked countries are at the mercy of their coastal neighbors, on whom they depend for access to sea-based international trade.

A well-functioning African Union is therefore vital for Africa's escape from poverty and sustainable development. The EU is the most important role model for the AU, so that greater European aid and political support to Africa's integration would be strategic for Europe and welcome for Africa. Sub-Saharan Africa's development challenges are enormous, no doubt. Africa is the epicenter of global extreme poverty and remains bereft of basic infrastructure. It is highly vulnerable to global warming and to an exceedingly high fertility rate that is causing rapid population growth and heavy outlays on schooling, health care, and infrastructure just to keep up with the soaring population. To overcome these difficulties, regional integration will be especially important to promote trade, tap into Africa's vast stores of renewable energy, and create new business opportunities and decent livelihoods.

The Middle East is perhaps the world's most politically riven region, yet another area where regional cooperation is vital for development. It's not called the "middle" for nothing. The Middle East sits athwart Europe, Asia, and Africa; it is home to the world's three great monotheistic traditions, Judaism, Christianity, and Islam; it is home to around 70 percent of the world's oil reserves, making it a great prize during the past century for the world's superpowers, all hungry for primary energy resources; and it juxtaposes three great competing cultural heritages and ethnicities: Turks, Arabs, and Persians. Add in the meddling by European empires, especially the British and French, and then after World War II by the United States, and one has the recipe for political mischief leading to geopolitical madness and perpetual war.

I have long fantasized about the "ultimate" case of regional integration, with Turkey, Saudi Arabia, and Iran finally deciding that there is far more that unites the Turks, the Arabs, and the Persians, than truly divides them. Their recent history has been to play one superpower off against the other, looking to Britain or France to keep Russia away, or Russia to keep the United States at bay, and so on. How much better off they would be if they worked together to tell the great powers in unison to stay away, at least in military terms. These three regional powers could then work together building a new regional infrastructure, tapping the region's vast solar power, desalination needs, shipping routes, and biodiversity, as well as its young people who can harness the new information technologies. Stranger things have happened.

The need to decarbonize the world's energy system should be, in itself, a major impetus to strengthen regional integration not only in the Middle East but in all parts of the world. The largest sources of low-carbon energy such as wind, solar, hydro, geothermal, and ocean power are typically far from population centers, as they are situated in mountains and deserts, along tectonic plates, and offshore. One recurring energy solution, therefore, is to tap the high-quality, low-carbon energy at the source and carry it to population centers via long-distance transmission lines. Such long-distance transmission will very often cross international boundaries. My own home, New York City, is looking to tap Canada's vast potential for hydroelectric power through a high-voltage, direct-current line. California and Texas, similarly, could tap the massive solar potential of northern Mexico. Europe could tap the solar power and wind energy of North Africa and the Middle East. All of this requires a high level of political trust among neighbors, with supporting political, economic, and financial institutions.

Once again the concept of *subsidiarity*—that problems should be solved at the lowest feasible level of governance—comes into play. Regional groupings like the European Union should focus on truly regional problems, such as cross-country infrastructure, trade, and movements of people and capital. Problems like the delivery of social services can often be best solved in neighborhoods, communities, or metropolitan regions. Cities have an important role to play in building codes, zoning, and local infrastructure such as charging points for electric vehicles. But national governments and regional organizations such as the European Union will need to attend to cross-border transmission of renewable energy, and global cooperation through the United Nations will be essential to set global goals and standards, such as in the Paris Climate Agreement.

In place of dead-end nationalism and warmongering exceptionalism, we should be strengthening regional groupings such as NAFTA, the European Union, the African Union, the Association of Southeast Asian Nations (ASEAN), and cooperation in northeast Asia among China, Japan, and South Korea. In every part of the world, sustainable development will depend on such regional cooperation. Yet such cooperation means moving beyond the conventional assumptions of balance-of-power politics, in which Saudi Arabia "must" compete with Iran, Japan with China, India with Pakistan, and so on. If these neighbors would cooperate rather than compete, they would strengthen their own nations, enhance the region's security, and contribute markedly to building global peace.

Part IV

RENEWING AMERICAN
DIPLOMACY

American exceptionalism has led to America's growing rejection of cooperative solutions and diplomatic approaches to global challenges. For the past quarter-century, the United States has turned its back on almost all UN treaties, refusing to sign or ratify several important agreements reached by all or almost all other UN member states. We have gone from being the creator and inspirer of the United Nations to a rogue nation that rejects UN initiatives for the perverse reason that most other nations endorse them.

American aloofness and often outright hostility to diplomacy comes at an odd time. The world community has recently shown that it can agree on many important matters. The most important global agreements in recent years are Agenda 2030, which commits all nations to sustainable development and the seventeen Sustainable Development Goals (17 SDGs), and the Paris Climate Agreement, which commits all nations to work cooperatively toward limiting global warming to "well below 2 degrees Celsius." Recent experience also points to the high returns from well-designed and well-targeted development assistance, which in recent years has proven its worth in fighting diseases such as AIDS, tuberculosis (TB), and malaria.

In this section I suggest that the United States would benefit enormously by adopting a UN-oriented foreign policy, one that aims to bolster the UN Charter and the work of UN institutions rather than resist them. Global cooperation can prevent or end wars through cooperative diplomacy in the UN Security Council, while sustainable development can be promoted through the 17 SDGs and the remarkable work of UN specialized agencies.

In the final chapter, I summarize ten major steps to creating a new U.S. foreign policy based on diplomacy and sustainable development. Such a foreign policy is our best chance for true security, enhanced well-being, and a better world for coming generations.

15

FROM DIPLOMATIC LEADER
TO ROGUE NATION

When America really was first, notably in the 1940s–1960s, America promoted its interests by cooperating with other nations. The United States opened its markets to the exports of Europe, Japan, and South Korea and shared American know-how with the least developed countries—for example, by promoting the Green Revolution in India in the 1960s. The United States developed the blueprints for the United Nations, the International Monetary Fund, the World Bank, the General Agreement on Tariffs and Trade (GATT, the forerunner of the World Trade Organization), the World Health Organization, the regional development banks, and countless other international efforts aimed at spreading economic prosperity.

The point is not that these actions were purely altruistic, imposing costs on the United States that only helped other countries. The point, rather, is that the United States invested in global public goods—in win-win activities—knowing that by playing its part, even a disproportionate part, as the world's leading economy and military power, it would reap a significant long-term benefit along with the other nations. Leadership does not mean squeezing other nations to enrich one's own country. Leadership is finding opportunities for mutual gain and creatively pursuing them, even funding projects entirely at times, when all countries end up ahead.

President John F. Kennedy famously put the issue of development assistance this way in his inaugural address:

> To those peoples in the huts and villages across the globe struggling to break the bonds of mass misery, we pledge our best efforts to help them help themselves, for whatever period is required—not because the Communists may be doing it, not because we seek their votes, but because it is right. If a free society cannot help the many who are poor, it cannot save the few who are rich.

America's efforts can be measured by official development aid (ODA) as a share of gross national income (GNI), as shown in figure 15.1. During the Marshall Plan years, U.S. aid levels were about 1 percent of U.S. gross domestic product (GDP, almost the same as GNI). During the 1950s, the aid levels trended downward, but were still on the order of 0.6 percent of GDP in the early 1960s. This fell further to 0.2–0.3 percent in the 1970s and 1980s, then plummeted below 0.2 percent at the end of the Cold War, falling to 0.1 percent of GDP in 1999 during the Clinton administration. The aid levels increased under George W. Bush, who as we'll see made a notable effort to fight AIDS, TB, and malaria, with ODA/GNI rising to around 0.2. Under Obama the aid effort fell back again to around 0.18, and it looks set to fall further under Trump, perhaps to around 0.15.

This downward trend broadly tracks America's declining readiness to invest in global public goods generally. In the first decades after World War II—the heyday of the American

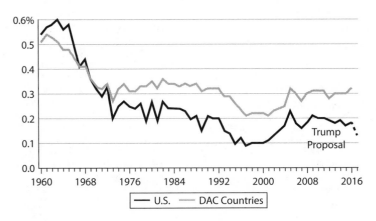

FIGURE 15.1 Official development assistance as a percentage of national income: United States versus all donor countries, 1960–2016. Data from Net ODA, OECD.org: https://data.oecd.org/oda /net-oda.htm.

Century—the United States was ready to lead in deeds as well as words. Representing around 30 percent of world GDP and more than half the combined income of the United States, Europe, and Japan, the United States not only was keen to promote the new U.S.-led internationalism, but also knew that positive results depended on America's footing much of the bill, admittedly to its own advantage as well as that of the countries receiving the aid.

Starting in the early 1970s, the United States began to pull back from global financial leadership. In 1971, President Richard Nixon unilaterally severed the fixed exchange rate between the U.S. dollar and gold (thirty-five dollars per ounce), thereby ending the "gold standard" of the postwar monetary system. The United States refused to bear the macroeconomic costs that would have been needed to preserve the dollar's peg to gold as was called for under the globally agreed monetary arrangements, and as was expected by other countries. The rest of the world, which was left holding dollar reserves that were now reduced in value, suffered the cost of Nixon's unilateral action. This action marked a watershed, a turning point in America's readiness to foot the bill for the global financial system.

America's will to leadership was further undermined by new developments in North-South diplomacy. The postcolonial nations made an appeal at the United Nations for a New International Economic Order (NIEO) that would ostensibly treat the developing countries more fairly—for example, by boosting the world relative price of primary commodities through methods such as export cartels and commodity stabilization arrangements. The developing countries began to claim, with increasing determination, that the existing international economic order was unfair to the late industrializers, and that the system needed to be reformed. If an oil cartel like OPEC could push up international prices, they reasoned, so too could cartels for products such as sugar, coffee, tobacco, cocoa, and others.

In the face of this call for global equity, the United States issued a resounding no. The international economic system, said one U.S. administration after the next, is fair enough. If developing countries wanted to catch up, they'd have to do it on their own, presumably by mastering new areas of technology and skill, not by artificial arrangements to boost the prices of their commodity exports. A few countries, such as South Korea and Singapore, were able to follow that route. Others, however, remained stuck with their traditional commodity exports and found their national income levels stagnant or declining as their populations grew while their terms of trade declined.

Just as significantly, the United States lost the political will to support the rapid catching-up of the developing countries.

The call for a NIEO was taken as an affront, an appeal to naïve socialism and redistribution, a violation of the principles of market competition. The fact that many of these same countries were involved in OPEC, the ascendant oil cartel, added to the sting of NIEO. The United States made clear that it had had enough. When developing countries fell into financial crisis in the early 1980s (following sky-high U.S. interest rates), the United States took a mostly hard-line position: repay the debts or suffer the consequences.

The U.S. will to lead globally had its final moment of glory in the postcommunist revolutions of 1989–1991. After all, the emergence of postcommunist governments in Eastern Europe was the triumph, or so it seemed, of decades of America's Cold War efforts. While America's generosity to the newly democratic nations of Eastern Europe can easily be exaggerated, the fact remains that the United States saw that investing in Eastern Europe's transformation, democratization, and renewed growth would enhance U.S. exports, geopolitical leadership, and returns on overseas investments.

I have already recounted the stark difference between America's financial approach toward Poland in 1989 and Russia in 1991. The first showed U.S. financial leadership, the other the abnegation of leadership. Yes, the United States still wanted to lead after 1991, but through military dominance over its former adversary rather than through cooperative economic strategies. Official development assistance generally plummeted in the 1990s. Clinton wanted a post–Cold War peace dividend without having to reinvest any of it abroad to build a new world order. With no geopolitical competition from the Soviet Union for the hearts and minds of the world's poor, the United States no longer had to use development assistance as an inducement for countries to join the U.S. sphere of influence.

I therefore see several reasons for America's shrinking interest in global economic, financial, and diplomatic leadership. One was petulance. The United States was annoyed by demands for global economic reform coming from the developing countries; they would take the global system on America's terms, or else. Another was the end of the Cold War. The United States had won; the Soviet Union had lost. The United States no longer needed to lure developing countries to its side and away from the Soviet Union. A third was arrogance. Why lead with inducements (carrots) when military power (sticks) will do just fine? The United States turned from "soft" power to "hard" power after 1991, especially since the Soviet Union was no longer present as a military counterweight (or so the United States thought, until Russia's intervention in Syria in 2015).

Perhaps most fundamental of all, and underpinning some of the factors just named, was America's relative decline in economic strength. The U.S. economy did not fail; much of the world caught up, or at least narrowed the gap. Europe and Japan rebuilt after the war. Developing countries invested in education and job skills. China experienced the most rapid, sustained economic growth of any large region in the world after market reforms began in 1978. The result was that America's share of world output fell from its peak of around 30 percent in 1950 to 20 percent by 1990 and just 15 percent today. As the U.S. share declined, America's readiness to supply global public goods fell even faster. And because the American political system after 1980 failed to redistribute wealth and income from the top to the bottom, a significant part of the U.S. population experienced an absolute decline in inflation-adjusted income, despite the overall growth of the U.S. economy.

Yet here is where America has badly misjudged its own situation and the world's. While it is understandable that the United States would no longer bankroll global development as it did in the 1940s–1950s, the need for global public goods has not abated just because U.S. economic dominance has diminished. The global needs remain, for example, to fight global poverty and battle human-induced climate change. Rather than turning its back on such global challenges, the United States should be calling on other nations to join with it in meeting the challenges together. Instead, the United States has abdicated its responsibilities by slashing aid, relying excessively on hard power, and renouncing the instruments of global diplomacy.

Not only has the United States turned its back on development assistance; it has turned its back on global diplomacy as well. The United Nations was America's creation, the remarkable vision of Franklin D. Roosevelt as the best hope to keep the peace after World War II. So too was the web of new international institutions within and alongside the United Nations. U.S. diplomats seemed to be everywhere for the first quarter-century after the war, helping to launch development programs, instill environmentalism, and share the fruits of science. But then, for the same reasons that the United States cut back on global development financing, it began to cut back on global diplomacy as well. The bipartisan foreign policy of the Roosevelt-Truman-Eisenhower era increasingly gave way to dissension. Hard-liners decided that U.S. military dominance, rather than diplomatic persuasion and development financing, was the real key to securing America's interests.

From the late 1970s onward, international treaties became increasingly suspect to the American right wing. Since 1994, the U.S. Senate has not ratified a single UN treaty, the last being the Chemical Weapons Convention in 1993. Ratification requires a two-thirds majority, implying bipartisan support, and generally the Republican Party has stood nearly united against ratification. Here are some of the important UN treaties pending Senate ratification, with few if any prospects for adoption:

1979 Convention on the Elimination of All Forms of Discrimination Against Women, signed but not ratified

1989 Convention on the Rights of the Child, signed but not ratified

1989 Basel Convention on Transboundary Hazardous Wastes, signed but not ratified

1991 United Nations Convention on the Law of the Sea, not signed

1992 Convention on Biological Diversity, signed but not ratified

1996 Comprehensive Test Ban Treaty, signed but not ratified

1997 Kyoto Protocol, signed with no intention to ratify

1997 Ottawa Treaty (Mine Ban Treaty), not signed

1998 Rome Statute of the International Criminal Court, not signed

1999 Criminal Law Convention on Corruption, signed but not ratified

1999 Civil Law Convention on Corruption, not signed

2002 Optional Protocol to the Convention Against Torture, not signed

2006 International Convention for the Protection of All Persons from Enforced Disappearance, not signed

2007 Convention on the Rights of Persons with Disabilities, signed but not ratified

2015 Paris Climate Agreement, signed but declared intention to withdraw in 2020

In many of these cases, the United States stands alone or almost alone against the rest of the world. Only four countries have failed to ratify the convention on elimination of discrimination against women (CEDAW)—the United States plus Somalia, Sudan, and Iran. Only the United States is not a party to the Convention on the Rights of the Child. Only the United States is not a party to the Convention on Biological Diversity. Almost all countries have ratified the Convention on the Rights of Persons with Disabilities; the United States stands with Uzbekistan, Libya, Chad, Belarus, and a few others in not ratifying that treaty.

During the last quarter-century, the Republican Party has completely turned its back on global environmentalism, largely because the coal, oil, and gas lobbies came to dominate the party. In 1992, Republican president George H. W. Bush signed three major multilateral environmental agreements (MEAs) at the Rio Earth Summit: the Convention on Biological Diversity, the UN Framework Convention on Climate Change, and the UN Convention to Combat Desertification. Yet that proved the be the last gasp of Republican Party environmentalism. Since then, the U.S. Senate has turned its back on the treaties and on related global environmental measures.

Regarding the UN Convention on Biological Diversity (CBD), the Senate simply refused ratification after Bush signed the treaty. Several western-state Republican senators argued that protecting biodiversity under the treaty would undermine private property rights. In the end, private land rights took precedence over the survival of biodiversity.

Regarding the UN Framework Convention on Climate Change (UNFCCC), the Senate ratified the treaty but then refused to implement it, and likewise refused to consider the 1997 Kyoto Protocol that would have put the treaty into

operation. The 2015 Paris Climate Agreement has now super-
seded the Kyoto Protocol. The agreement was designed by the
Obama administration and other negotiating partners to cir-
cumvent the need for Senate ratification. Instead, the Republican Senate leadership successfully convinced President Trump
to announce plans to withdraw from the agreement in 2020,
the earliest possible date under the terms of the agreement.

Regarding the UN Convention to Combat Desertification
(UNCCD), the Senate ratified the treaty but did absolutely
nothing to support it. The aim of the UNCCD is to support
dryland countries to confront and overcome the scourges of
drought and land degradation. Dryland regions such as the
African Sahel, the Horn of Africa, the Arabian Gulf, and
Western and Central Asia, are exceedingly vulnerable to global
warming and the overuse of surface water and groundwater.
The dryland regions have become conflict hotspots in part
because of food and water insecurity. Yet the United States
has not utilized the UNCCD as an instrument of response,
turning to military approaches instead.

With Trump's presidency, the United States is completing
the move from postwar leader to twenty-first-century rogue
state. Trump is not just cutting aid and rejecting global treaties. He is undermining UN diplomacy itself. Trump and
UN ambassador Nikki Haley have taken delight in thumbing
their noses at UN diplomats, with Haley declaring repeatedly
that "we are taking down names" of countries that oppose the
United States, and threatening to cut aid to countries that
cross the United States diplomatically.

Trump and Haley have already made good on their threat
to cut funding to the UN itself; on Christmas Eve 2017,
America's gift to the world was a $285 million cut in the United
Nations' regular budget. Technically, the UN regular budget

reflects a consensus decision of the body's 193 member states, but the United States was clearly the prime mover in pushing for the cut. Indeed, Nikki Haley, the U.S. ambassador to the UN, accompanied the Christmas Eve announcement with a warning that the United States would be on the lookout for further reductions.

The budget cuts will make it that much harder for UN agencies to prevent wars, help millions of people displaced by conflicts, feed and clothe hungry children, fight emerging diseases, provide safe water and sanitation, and promote access to education and health care for the poor.

President Trump and Ambassador Haley make much of the bloated costs of UN operations, and there certainly is room for some trimming. But the world receives an astounding return on its investments in the UN, and member countries should be investing far more, not less, in the organization and its programs.

Consider the sums. The UN regular budget for the two-year period 2018–2019 will stand at around $5.3 billion, $285 million less than the 2016–2017 budget. Annual spending will be around $2.7 billion. The U.S. share will be 22 percent, or around $580 million per year, equivalent to around $1.80 per American per year.

What will Americans get for their $1.80 per year? For starters, the UN regular budget includes the operations of the General Assembly, the Security Council, and the Secretariat (including the secretary-general's office, the Department of Economic and Social Affairs, the Department of Political Affairs, and administrative staff). When a dire threat to peace arises, such as the current standoff between the United States and North Korea, it is the UN's Department of Political Affairs that often facilitates vital, behind-the-scenes diplomacy.

In addition, the UN regular budget includes allocations for the UN Children's Fund (UNICEF), the UN Development Program, the World Health Organization, the UN High Commissioner for Refugees, the UN High Commissioner for Human Rights, the UN's regional bodies (for Asia, Africa, Europe, Latin America), the UN Environment Program, the Office for the Coordination of Humanitarian Affairs (for disaster response), the World Meteorological Organization, the UN Office on Drugs and Crime, UN Women (for women's rights), and many other agencies, each specializing in global responses to crises, conflicts, poverty, displacement, environmental hazards, diseases, or other public needs.

Many UN organizations receive additional "voluntary" contributions from individual countries interested in supporting specialized initiatives by agencies such as UNICEF and the World Health Organization. Those agencies have a unique global mandate and political legitimacy, and the capacity to operate in all parts of the world.

The silliness of the U.S. attack on the size of the UN budget is best seen by, once again, comparing it to the Pentagon's budget. The United States currently spends around $700 billion per year on defense, or roughly $2 billion per day. Thus, the total annual UN regular budget amounts to around one day and nine hours of U.S. military spending. The U.S. share of the UN regular budget equals roughly seven hours of Pentagon spending. Some waste.

Trump and Haley are squeezing the UN budget for three reasons. The first is to play to Trump's political base. Most Americans recognize the enormous value of the UN and support it, but the right-wing fringe among Republican voters views the UN as an affront to the United States. A 2016 Pew survey put U.S. public approval of the UN at 64 percent, with just 29 percent viewing it unfavorably.[1] Yet the Texas Republican Party, for example, has repeatedly called on the United States to leave the UN.

The second reason is to save on wasteful programs, which is necessary in any ongoing organization. The mistake is to slash the overall budget, rather than reallocate funds and increase outlays on vitally needed programs that fight hunger and disease, educate children, and prevent conflicts.

The third, and most dangerous, reason for cutting the UN's budget is to weaken multilateralism in the name of American "sovereignty." The United States is sovereign, Trump and Haley insist, and therefore can do what it wants, regardless of opposition by the UN or any other group of countries.

This attitude was on display in Haley's speech to the UN General Assembly session on Jerusalem. The UN Security Council had voted fourteen to one against the United States to oppose Trump's moving the U.S. embassy to Jerusalem; countries friendly to the United States and Israel warned vigorously that Trump's move not only violated international law but would threaten the peace process. The UN General Assembly also took up the issue, voting 128 to nine against the United States, with thirty-five abstentions, despite harsh U.S. warnings of aid cutoffs. Haley told the rest of the world:

> America will put our embassy in Jerusalem. That is what the American people want us to do, and it is the right thing to do. No vote in the United Nations will make any difference on that. But this vote will make a difference on how Americans look at the UN and on how we look at countries who disrespect us in the UN. And this vote will be remembered.[2]

This approach to sovereignty is exceedingly risky. Most obviously, it repudiates international law. In the case of Jerusalem, resolutions adopted by the General Assembly and the Security Council have repeatedly declared the final status of Jerusalem to be a matter of international law. By brazenly proclaiming the right to override international law, the United States threatens the edifice of international cooperation under the UN Charter.

Yet another grave danger is to the United States itself. When America stops listening to other countries, its vast military power and arrogance often lead to self-inflicted disasters. America Firsters like Trump and Haley bristle when other countries oppose U.S. foreign policy; but these other countries are usually giving the United States their good and frank advice that the United States would be very wise to heed. The Security Council's opposition to the U.S.-led war in Iraq in 2003, for example, wasn't intended to weaken America, but to protect the United States, Iraq, and indeed the world, from America's rage and shocking blindness to the facts.

How the rest of the world might react to such posturing by the United States is clear from the Turkish foreign minister's succinct rejoinder to Haley: "Dignity and sovereignty are not for sale."[3] The United States can continue to be a bully and to go its own way, but the world will not give in.

16

THE ETHICS AND PRACTICALITIES
OF FOREIGN AID

A s a lifelong advocate for development aid for the world's poor, I am angered by the repeated attempts by the Trump administration to slash U.S. foreign aid. So far, the largest of the proposed cuts have been resisted by the Senate, including Republican Senators who know better. They know how many children would die or grow up without access to education if President Trump's proposals were to be adopted. Moreover, the financial savings for the United States would be trivial, but the costs to millions of impoverished people would be enormous. The total aid budget is around $31 billion, roughly two weeks of Pentagon spending.

Even worse, the cuts in aid are explicitly designed to help shift funding toward an increase in military spending, one that is utterly unnecessary and that in any event should not be funded on the backs of the world's poorest people. Instead of cutting development aid to fund an increase in military spending, we should be ending wars and spending on new weapons systems precisely to increase aid for health, education, renewable energy, and infrastructure, as well as urgently needed spending at home.

Trump's calls for cutting foreign aid will surely appeal to his base, who are told that the aid is coming out of their own pockets, whereas it is the tax cuts for the rich and the endless wars that are really fleecing the working class. Cuts in foreign aid would cause enormous harm to America's well-being, not only to our nation's moral standards, but to American national security and jobs as well.

My own support for foreign assistance is based on morality. "Justice, justice shall you pursue," we are told in the book of Deuteronomy. Those who fail to help the poor cast themselves outside of the moral community. "For I was hungry and you gave me nothing to eat, I was thirsty and you gave me nothing to drink, I was a stranger and you did not invite me in, I needed clothes and you did not clothe me, I was sick and in prison and you did not look after me," warns Jesus in the Gospel of Matthew.

Charity (*zakat*) is a bedrock of Islam. Compassion is the very core of Buddhism. Indeed, for all systems of morals, both religious and secular, treating others as we would be treated is the very essences of morality. If my own children were hungry, without medicine, or without schooling, I would desperately want them to be helped. Our responsibility is equally clear. Moreover, I believe, along with the teachings of the ancient prophets, that a nation built on iniquity cannot long survive. It will come apart at the seams, as America may be doing today.

I also know, as a development practitioner now for thirty-two years, that foreign aid works—when we put in the honest effort and thinking to make it work. I am not talking about the kind of U.S. aid that is handed over to warlords, as in Iraq and Afghanistan. I'd cut out that aid in a moment. I'm not talking about aid that is handed out by the U.S. military. I do not believe in the Pentagon's and the CIA's campaigns for "hearts and minds," designed by people whose real training lies not in providing public health, but in killing. And I'm not talking about the aid delivered largely by American expatriates in somebody else's country. Almost all local service delivery should be carried out by locals except in exceptional circumstances (e.g., in the immediate aftermath of natural disasters when all hands are needed).

Aid works when its main purpose is to finance supplies such as medicines and solar panels and the staffing is by local workers in public health, agronomy, hydrology, ecology, energy, and transport. U.S. government aid should be pooled with funds from other governments to support critical investments in health, education, agriculture, and infrastructure, based on professional best practices. That's how the Global Fund to Fight AIDS, Tuberculosis, and Malaria works, as one important example. It's a model of success, having saved 22 million lives from the three diseases, according to its *Results Report 2017*.

This kind of aid is not "the white man's burden," as has been alleged. The responsibility to help the poor is carried by no race for any other race. It is about the rich doing what they should for the poor. "From everyone to whom much has been given, much will be required," says Jesus in the Gospel of Luke.

Nor is good aid about "the poor in the rich countries helping the rich in the poor countries," as foes of aid have long quipped. When aid funds are directed toward the basics—safe childbirth; immunizations; control of diarrheal diseases, malaria, and HIV/AIDS; irrigation for smallholder farmers; information and communications technologies for e-governance, e-finance, e-education, and e-health; ensuring access to schooling; protecting biodiversity; and restoring degraded lands— the beneficiaries will be the poor. And as long as the United

States maintains fairness in its tax system, the rich will be bearing their fair share. It is true that a politically viable aid program goes hand in hand with a fair tax system.

There is a lot of negative propaganda about foreign aid, since foreign aid is an easy target. There are very few knowledgeable people around to defend it, and the recipients it keeps alive don't vote in U.S. elections. We certainly hear an earful: aid is wasted; aid is a huge budgetary burden; aid demeans the recipients; aid is no longer needed in the twenty-first-century. In short, we are told that aid does not work.

The simple fact is that some aid is wasted and other aid is used brilliantly. The main issue is whether the aid directly supports the work of local professionals saving lives, growing food, installing rural electricity, and teaching children, or whether the aid goes instead to foreign warlords or overpriced American companies. Our responsibility is to fund the aid that works and, when this has been demonstrated, as in public health and education, to expand the assistance as needed by the poorest of the poor.

Aid is a only around 1 percent of the federal budget, and less than one-fifth of 1 percent of national income. It is twenty-five times smaller than the outlays on the military (adding together the Pentagon, intelligence agencies, nuclear weapons programs, veterans' outlays, and other military-linked spending). And as Trump himself has acknowledged, military spending has squandered many trillions of dollars in Middle East wars that have only exacerbated global threats and U.S. insecurity.

As we saw in the previous chapter, a country's aid effort is usually measured by its official development assistance (ODA) relative to its gross national income (GNI, similar to GDP). While the United States gives more aid than any other country in absolute terms, this is because the United

States is by far the largest economy among the traditional donor countries in the Organization for Economic Cooperation and Development (OECD). Back in 1971, the UN General Assembly called upon all donor nations to spend at least 0.7 percent of their GNI on official development assistance. The United States is now below 0.2 percent, placing the U.S. aid effort among the lowest of all donor countries, a point made clear by comparing the ODA/GNI ratios for the twenty-nine OECD donor nations (figure 16.1). In 2016, the United States ranked twenty-second out of twenty-nine donors, at 0.18 percent of GNI (roughly $33.6 billion out of $18.6 trillion).

One phony charge is that aid is demeaning. Nothing could be further from the truth. Aid enables HIV-infected mothers to stay alive and raise their children. Demeaning? Aid enables a child in an impoverished country to escape death or permanent brain damage from malaria, a 100 percent treatable disease. Demeaning? Aid enables a poor child to go to a school fitted with computers, solar power, and wireless connectivity. Demeaning?

Aid is definitely needed still, albeit by a smaller and smaller share of the world. In the 1940s, aid was vital for Europe; hence the Marshall Plan. By the 1950s, Europe had "graduated" from aid; the focus was on Latin America and parts of Asia. Most of those countries too have long since graduated. Aid today should focus on the countries that are still poor—roughly the one billion or so people in the low-income countries and the poorest of the middle-income countries. With open world markets, improved technologies, and a boost from adequate aid flows for health, education, agriculture, and infrastructure, these remaining countries too could graduate from aid by around 2030.

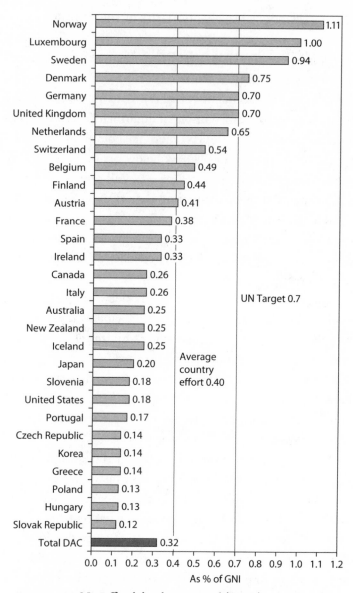

FIGURE 16.1 Net official development aid (ODA) as a percentage of gross national income (GNI), 2016

Source: Organization for Economic Cooperation and Development (OECD), "Development Aid Rises Again in 2016," April 11, 2017, https://www.oecd.org/dac/financing-sustainable-development/development-finance-data/ODA-2016-detailed-summary.pdf.

Another myth is that the United States carries the aid burden while other governments shirk their responsibility. This is plain wrong. In 2016, the ODA/GNI ratio of the European Union, for example, was 0.51, roughly three times the aid effort of America's 0.18. Combining all of the non-U.S. OECD donor countries, the ratio of ODA to GNI stood at 0.42, more than twice the U.S. aid effort.

The best aid giver among our last three presidents was George W. Bush. Thanks to Bush's leadership, aid under his presidency saved millions of lives of HIV-infected people around the world. It saved hundreds of thousands of lives of young children who would otherwise die of malaria. It spared America the ravages of disease epidemics that would start abroad and then hit the U.S. shores. It fed hungry and threatened populations displaced by typhoons, floods, droughts, famines, and conflicts.

By contrast, Bill Clinton and Barack Obama did very little during their presidencies. Obama's main contribution was to continue Bush's programs but without funding the growing needs. Trump, alas, seems prepared to trash the aid budget entirely if he gets his way. Does this mean the American people turn our backs on America's long-standing and successful efforts to fight killer diseases, hunger, and extreme poverty?

The moral justification of aid, as powerful and adequate as it is, is matched by an equally important case of self-interest. Aid is a matter of U.S. national security and economic interest.

Regarding the links between aid and national security, there is no need to listen to a moralizing economist. Listen directly to the generals. More than 120 retired generals and admirals recently wrote to the congressional leaders of both parties to defend aid as a critical bulwark of national security:

The State Department, USAID, Millennium Challenge Corporation, Peace Corps, and other development agencies are critical to preventing conflict and reducing the need to put our men and women in uniform in harm's way. As Secretary James Mattis said while commander of US Central Command, "If you don't fully fund the State Department, then I need to buy more ammunition." The military will lead the fight against terrorism on the battlefield, but it needs strong civilian partners in the battle against the drivers of extremism—lack of opportunity, insecurity, injustice, and hopelessness.[1]

For this reason, Senator Lindsay Graham of South Carolina has said of the Trump proposal to slash aid: "It's dead on arrival, it's not going to happen, it would be a disaster. This budget destroys soft power, it puts our diplomats at risk, and it's going nowhere."

What is especially foolish about the Trump proposal is that the United States would be slashing its own aid precisely when China is ramping up its aid. China is signing and financing major development projects across Southeast Asia, South Asia, Central Asia, Western Asia, and Africa. China may already be the world's largest aid giver. Trump's plans would accelerate the transition to China's preeminence. Who will find diplomatic support in the next global crisis, China or the United States? And whose companies will win the next round of major infrastructure projects? Both the United States and China can and should do their part.

So too, I must add, should the world's billionaires. Governments have cut the taxes of the rich so much, and so catered to their needs, that we should now be turning to this vast accumulation of private wealth to contribute to global needs alongside governments. These two thousand billionaires, realistically, can and should be providing tens of billions of dollars of annual contributions toward the Sustainable Development Goals. I take up that issue in chapter 18.

We must ultimately acknowledge another more radical, and more accurate, perspective: this is not aid at all, but justice. There are two senses in which "aid" is absolutely the wrong word when it comes to helping the world's poor.

The first returns us to morality. In his wonderful encyclical "Populorum Progressio" (1967), Pope Paul VI noted this of giving to the poor: "As St. Ambrose put it: 'You are not making a gift of what is yours to the poor man, but you are giving him back what is his. You have been appropriating things that are meant to be for the common use of everyone. The Earth belongs to everyone, not to the rich.' "

This idea of "appropriating things that are meant to be for the common use" is appropriate in a dramatically literal sense as well. The rich countries, including our own, have long robbed and despoiled the planet for our narrow economic gain. Britain, the United States, and other powers have made a career of stealing the oil, gas, and minerals out from under the sands of other nations. Our countries transported millions of African slaves to work the plantations stolen from indigenous populations. Our multinational companies have routinely bribed foreign leaders for land and oil reserves. The U.S. government has launched dozens of coups and wars to secure oil, gas, copper, banana and sugar plantations, and other valuable resources. Our fishing fleets have illegally and recklessly scoured the seas, including the protected economic zones of the poorest countries. And our reckless emissions of greenhouse gases are directly responsible for droughts, floods, and extreme storms around the world, with a president and oil industry too evil even to acknowledge the basic scientific truths.

At very low cost, the United States together with partner countries could help to end the HIV/AIDS epidemic. Building on Bush's innovative steps fifteen years ago, and many new technologies, Trump could partner with other countries to prevent nearly all new infections of HIV. Similarly, building on the long-standing commitments of the United States and other countries, a modest increase of aid would ensure that every girl and boy in the poorest countries can stay in school through high school. In that way, impoverished children would not end up as child soldiers or as unemployed youth who are easily radicalized.

Yet despite the urgent need to look outward and fight issues like disease, poverty, and climate change that vex the world, we are turning inward. We do not want to help those outside our borders, nor do we want those who need help to cross our borders. The folly of this mind-set is the subject of the next chapter.

17

MANAGING MIGRATION

Donald Trump's various efforts to bar entry to the United States from Muslim-majority countries is the latest salvo in America's epic culture wars over race and American identity. As a matter of national security and law, Trump's proposals have not passed legal muster. Several judges have overturned part or all of his various executive orders, though the legal battles continue to the Supreme Court. Yet Trump has figured that he wins politically even when he loses in court. Trump's politics depend on making Muslims a target of hatred among working-class white voters, a strategy with a long and successful history in U.S. politics.

Viewed from a national security perspective, Trump's various entry bans have failed the credibility test. As several federal courts have pointed out, not a single terrorist attack in the United States has involved a visa-holder from the six Muslim countries named in the original travel ban (Iran, Libya, Somalia, Sudan, Syria, and Yemen, with Iraq included at the outset but then removed from subsequent versions of the executive order). In fact, 9/11 was carried out by Saudis, and most of the other terrorist attacks have been carried out by U.S. citizens. A draft report by the Department of Homeland

Security itself noted that citizenship is an "unlikely indicator" of terrorist threats. Some observers have noted that the various versions of the Muslim travel ban have skipped Muslim-majority countries where Trump has business interests. Trump himself claims that the list of countries came from the Obama administration, but the Obama administration list was merely to require visas for individuals who had recently visited one of the countries, not to bar entry by nationals of those countries.

Trump's real purpose isn't antiterrorism at all. The real goal is to fan the perception among Trump's political base that Islam is an existential threat to Western civilization and that allowing Muslims to enter the United States would be to permit radical terrorist cells to grow inside the United States. Trump said as much in his first address to a joint session of Congress: "We cannot allow a beachhead of terrorism to form inside America, and we cannot allow our nation to become a sanctuary for extremists."[1]

For many Americans, including myself, this seems like a vulgarity. It is outrageous for the president to conflate refugees escaping from a war-torn region, or scientists and students visiting the United States on short-term visits or student visas, with terrorists forming a beachhead. It is even more hateful to do so when the United States has been the key instigator of the wars that the refugees are trying to flee. The United States has launched five major wars in the Middle East since 1990 (two in Iraq and one each in Afghanistan, Libya, and Syria) and is fighting in countless smaller wars (in Yemen and Somalia, among other places). Yet the United States has the audacity to close the doors to any and all victims of the violence.

Trump's moves are about identity, emotion, and politics, not logic, national security, and the law. For many Americans, 9/11 is a continuing trauma, fanned by repeated viewing of the horrors in the media. Psychological research shows that repeated viewings of the 9/11 and Iraq War carnage have been associated with adverse mental health consequences—a media-induced posttraumatic stress. Trump is playing straight to that trauma. We recall that in the immediate aftermath of 9/11, many Americans, including the Bush White House, were uninterested as to whether Saddam Hussein had been part of 9/11. Trauma was trauma, and the United States needed to respond with war, against somebody.

There is plenty of evidence regarding the exaggerated fears around Islam. Many Americans now believe that America is being overrun with Muslims. Ask yourself the question: What share of the U.S. population is Muslim? Americans, on average, guess 17 percent. The correct answer is around 1 percent.

Trump is mining that deep vein of fear and hate. His message plays especially well among white working-class men, Trump's base.

American attitudes toward Islam vary strongly with educational attainment. College-educated Americans, who tended to vote against Trump, see Islam favorably, while Americans with less than a college education, Trump's base, tend to see Islam unfavorably. In a 2010 Pew survey, for example, the favorable-unfavorable divide was 47–28 among college grads; 29–37 among those with some college but no degree; and 20–45 among those with a high school diploma.

The fact that more-educated individuals harbor less negative views of Islam is a familiar pattern found in social psychology. Education generally breaks down us-versus-them stereotypes. More education also makes one's job prospects more secure, so better-educated Americans have less fear of losing their wages or jobs to immigrants.

In playing to his base, Trump is of course tapping into one of the most familiar motifs of American history: the visceral fear that the white working class has long held for nonwhite immigrants. Such fears are reaching a new crescendo as the United States shifts from being a majority-white (non-Hispanic) society to a white-minority society. According to the Census Bureau, by around 2044 the white, non-Hispanic population will become less than half of the total population for the first time in the nation's history. The goal of white nationalists, a part of Trump's base, is to promote immigration bans, deportations, heavy police tactics, and other fearmongering to try to shift this demographic trend before it is "too late" for the white, non-Hispanic majority.

The long history of the United States is of two white classes, a rich elite (one that originally included the slave-owning class) and a hardscrabble working class that takes solace in its social status remaining above that of even more desperate African Americans, Native Americans, and other minorities. Rich whites have long sought the political allegiance of poor whites by promising to keep minority groups from rising too far, too fast in economic, social, and political terms. The goal of the elites has been to forestall a class-based politics in which poor whites and poor minority groups actually join together to demand redistribution from the rich. In this the rich have been remarkably cynical and remarkably successful. (In a perverse way, the elites of *both* political parties have tended to favor distinctive brands of identity politics over class politics to divert attention from the massive inequalities of income and wealth in American society.)

It is no accident that the very first naturalization legislation of the United States, the 1790 Naturalization Act, limited naturalized citizenship to "free white persons of good character," thereby excluding Africans, Native Americans, and, later, Asians. Forty years later, in 1830, Andrew Jackson, the president to whom Trump is most often compared in terms of personality and temperament, signed the Indian Removal Act. This act began the ethnic cleansing of the southeastern United States (east of the Mississippi) with the forced resettlement of the Cherokee Nation along the deadly Trail of Tears to Oklahoma. Poor white farmers as well as large landowners (including Jackson himself) grabbed the land dispossessed from the departing Cherokee. Thousands of Cherokees died in this act of stunning barbarity and cruelty. These expulsions were followed by further acts of war and genocide, until the Native populations were entirely conquered or eliminated by the end of the nineteenth century.

In 1882, President Chester Arthur signed the China Exclusion Act, designed to prevent the "yellow hordes" of Asia from becoming the next threat to the white homeland. The act barred Chinese "skilled and unskilled laborers and Chinese employed in mining." Chinese families were divided between those in the United States and those still in China. Chinese living in the United States who sought to visit their families in China were told that they would not be allowed to return. Senator George Frisbie Hoar of Massachusetts declared the act to be "nothing less than the legalization of racial discrimination."

The Chinese Exclusion Act was a watershed, as it opened up more than eighty years of immigration policy based on the national origin of immigrants, a policy not unlike Trump's travel ban. By the early 1900s, the racial fears shifted from Chinese immigration, now suppressed, to Jews and rural poor flooding in from Eastern and Southern Europe. This new immigration was squelched by the 1924 Immigration Act, which established immigration quotas according to national origin, with the number of immigrants allowed from each country based on the number of foreign-born residents in the United States as of 1890.

For the years 1925–1927, for example, the total number of immigrants was capped at 164,667 arrivals, roughly one-fifth of the annual immigrant arrivals in the period before World War I. Of those 164,667 slots, 86.5 percent were reserved for Northern European immigrants, with more than half of that total reserved for immigrants from Germany and the United Kingdom. Only 11.2 percent of the total could come from Southern and Eastern Europe. The number of migrants from all the rest of the world, including Latin America, Africa, and Asia, was capped at just 3,745 per year, or 2.3 percent of the total.

The 1924 Immigration Act, in short, achieved two goals: first, to reduce dramatically the total number of new immigrants, and second, to ensure that almost 90 percent of the immigrants allowed into the United States were from Northern Europe.

During this process, there was an attentive and approving observer abroad. Adolf Hitler praised the new U.S. immigration policy in *Mein Kampf*, writing, among other things:

> There is currently one state in which one can observe at least weak beginnings of a better conception. This is of course not our exemplary German Republic, but the American Union, in which an effort is being made to consider the dictates of reason to at least some extent. The American Union categorically refuses the immigration of physically unhealthy elements, and simply excludes the immigration of certain races. In these respects, America already pays obeisance, at least in tentative first steps, to the characteristic *völkich* conception of the state.[2]

In fact, in the 1930s, Nazi lawyers looked to various aspects of U.S. racial legislation—including the immigration codes based on country of national origin, the second-class citizenship of African Americans, the noncitizenship of colonial subjects such as Filipinos and Puerto Ricans, and the nonnational status of Native Americans—as role models for Germany's race-based citizenship, which culminated in the Nuremberg Codes. This point has been valiantly, if painfully, documented by the Yale legal historian James Whitman in his new book, *Hitler's American Model: The United States and the Making of Nazi Race Law.* Whitman's point, of course, is not that the United States caused the Nazi crimes; it is that the U.S. racial approach resonated with the Nazi racists.

The 1924 Immigration Act mostly closed America's doors and kept them closed for decades, even when Europe's Jews were desperately pleading for entry to the United States to save their lives. It was not until the 1965 Immigration and Nationality Act that the United States eventually relented on national origin. In the revised framework, which has now been the core of U.S. immigration law for a half-century, those with family and personal connections, as well as special categories of immigrants, were added to the immigrant roster, and the overall number of immigrants per year was increased.

Not only did U.S. immigration increase markedly, but it also shifted from Northern Europe to Latin America and Asia. Overall, the foreign-born population of the United States, which had fallen from around 13 percent of total population in the 1920 census to a low of 4.7 percent in 1970, has now risen to around 14 percent of the U.S. population, with nearly 40 percent of the foreign-born now from Mexico and Central America.

Trump's appeal to the white working class has combined fear of Middle East terrorism with a white working-class backlash against the rising Hispanic population. He has added in China-bashing, as well as opposition to immigration from what he termed "shithole" countries such as Haiti and African nations. In the good old American tradition of the elite class, the one thing Trump has never suggested is that America's super-rich might somehow help America's poor. Fomenting fear is a lot cheaper for those elites.

Of course, the United States isn't alone in its focus on the supposed danger of new arrivals to the country. In Europe as well, immigration is the number one political issue. Passions are high, dangerously so. The stakes are high as well. Migrants are risking their lives, and dying, to escape from violence, poverty, and joblessness. How can we reconcile the flood of migrants with the stiff backlash in the receiving societies?

I propose a three-part approach. The first is to stop the conflicts that are currently causing millions of refugees to flee their homes. The second is to promote long-term economic development in the countries migrants are fleeing. The third is to adjust global policies to enshrine the freedom to migrate while also enabling societies to limit migration to moderate and manageable rates.

Two conflict zones in particular, the Middle East and Central America, account for the recent surge of refugees to Europe and the United States, respectively. In both regions, an urgently needed change of U.S. foreign policy could staunch this flow. Sadly, both regions have instead been destabilized by misguided U.S. policies.

The Middle East conflicts, as discussed in chapter 6, are U.S. wars of choice. The three largest conflicts in the region, in Iraq, Libya, and Syria, reflect the repeated U.S. resort to violent "regime change." In all three cases, the result has been open-ended conflict and the rise of violent jihadists. As a result, millions of refugees have been crossing the Mediterranean into Europe from departure points mainly in Turkey and Libya.

In Central America, as in the Middle East, lamebrain CIA schemes—such as the 1980s Contra wars, the 2004 Haiti coup against Jean-Bertrand Aristide, and the 2009 Honduran coup against Manuel Zelaya—have stoked violence and created pervasive instability. In addition, the so-called U.S. war on drugs, fought in many parts of Latin America, has fomented massive violence. An American public health crisis—the epidemic use of opiates—has been transmuted into open war south of the U.S. border.

Both the Middle East and Central America demonstrate a compelling case for demilitarizing U.S. foreign policy. Ending covert CIA operations in the Middle East, Central America, and Africa would immediately reduce the displacement of populations and flow of refugees. Facing the opiate epidemic for what it really is—a public health challenge caused by massive social inequalities and desperation within U.S. communities—would stop the Latin American drug wars, save lives, and enable Central Americans to live in peace while remaining in their own countries.

Of course, even without the CIA wars of choice and the misguided war on drugs, millions of people around the world will still want to migrate to the United States and Europe in search of jobs, higher living standards, and social benefits. They will also come to escape from environmental degradation and the dislocations caused by global warming.

The correct response is to promote sustainable development in countries of large-scale out-migration. People will want to remain in their homelands if they see a viable future for their children. The good news is that sustainable development is feasible, and promoting it would be much cheaper for the United States and Europe than pursuing more failed wars, which have already cost the United States trillions of dollars in the Middle East alone in the past fifteen years.

Yet U.S. foreign policy is disastrously imbalanced, as we've seen: Our total aid budget is equal to around two weeks of Pentagon spending. The reason is obvious. Washington politicians salivate over each new taxpayer-subsidized weapons sale, which brings in its wake new campaign contributions and jobs for recycled politicians. Fighting disease, illiteracy, and poverty simply doesn't provide the D.C. political class with the same returns.

Looking ahead, the migration pressures will intensify unless the world acts to slow, and soon to stop, human-made global warming. If we fail to fulfill the climate commitments made in Paris, many places in the world will become less habitable and, for some, even uninhabitable. Global warming causes declining food yields in the tropics, intensifying droughts in the dry lands of North Africa and the Middle East, an expanded transmission zone of tropical diseases, more intense cyclones in Southeast Asia, and rising sea levels and flooding in coastal regions.

In addition to ending useless wars and promoting sustainable development, the third part of migration policy should be to make the world safe for diversity and for ongoing migration. Every one of us is from a migrant family. Every one of us has ancestors, if not ourselves, who have been "strangers in a strange land." The reasons for migration will continue to be powerful and diverse in the future. Our global norms and policies should respect the human right to migrate, albeit within reasonable limits.

Countries are certainly right to police their borders, but at the same time they should keep an open door for moderate and manageable rates of in-migration. No country should be allowed to slam its doors shut (and none would be wise to do so, and thereby lose the benefits of diversity). And while countries may be justified in limiting some social benefits to new migrants (to keep fiscal costs manageable and to limit incentives for excessive migrant inflows), the United States and other countries should ensure that migrant children receive the health care, schooling, and nutrition they need for their healthy development.

Rather than instituting unconscionable bans on the basis of religion or nation of origin, we should be insisting that the United States remain an open society, welcoming students and visitors from all parts of the world; enabling migration, subject to law and in reasonable numbers per year, from all parts of the world; accepting refugees fleeing for their lives, until their homelands are restored to peace and they can return safely; and policing our borders so that we enjoy the benefits of a law-based, safe, and responsible immigration policy.

Like Canada, the United States should limit the number of long-term immigrants per year and enforce the limits, but the limits should be reasonable and nondiscriminatory against any single religion, and should balance several objectives: family unification, job skills, business opportunities and needs, geographical diversity, caregivers, hardship cases, and other considerations. The reason for limits is clear: without them, literally hundreds of millions, perhaps billions of people would decamp for the high-income countries. Still, limiting immigration should not mean zero immigration, nor immigration on the basis of disfavored religions, races, or regions. And the counterpart of limited migration is far more generous development assistance and sound environmental policies, to ensure that all parts of the world can be habitable and prosperous without the need for forced mass migration.

Canada sets a goal of around 300,000 new immigrants each year, roughly 0.85 percent of the population, allocated across several distinct objectives. For the United States, current arrivals per year are around 1.4 million, or roughly 0.43 percent of the population, about half the immigration rate aimed for by Canada. Whether the United States targets the lower or upper end of this range, it has the wherewithal to accept more refugees and to welcome people from all parts of the world.

America's Muslim and Hispanic populations are especially fearful these days. It's everyone's job as citizens to defend their rights, their safety, their dignity, and their well-being. The Jewish teaching reminds us of a vital truth: "You shall not oppress a stranger, for you know the feelings of the stranger, having yourselves been strangers in the land of Egypt."

In short, migration is not about building high walls but about creating a world in which people can live securely and prosperously in their own homelands, while still enjoying the freedom to migrate for personal reasons rather than in desperation. By viewing the migration crisis in a more holistic way, we will find true and lasting solutions rather than the demagogic ones now widely on offer.

18

ACHIEVING SUSTAINABLE
DEVELOPMENT

The world output in 2018, measured at international prices, will be approximately $134 trillion, according to projections by the International Monetary Fund. That is an average of $17,600 for each man, woman, and child on the planet. This sum is easily enough to end all poverty, to ensure universal access to health care and education, and to provide the investments needed for the transformation to environmental sustainability. We are rich as a planet. We have no shortage of resources whatsoever.

In September 2015, the world agreed to put sustainable development at the center of global economic cooperation, adopting Agenda 2030 with the seventeen Sustainable Development Goals (SDGs). A few weeks later, the world adopted the Paris Climate Agreement. Together, these constitute a globally agreed agenda, albeit one that the Trump administration has ignored (in the case of the SDGs) or disdained (in the case of the Paris Climate Agreement).

The SDGs call for a more balanced society, in which economic growth is accompanied by policies to ensure that the economic growth is widely shared and environmentally sustainable. The SDGs are described as the "triple bottom line" of economic, social, and environmental objectives.

It is sometimes claimed that the SDGs are too expensive. Poor countries, for example, will probably need an additional $100–200 billion per year in development aid to meet the challenges of health, education, and basic infrastructure. That amount may seem unattainable, but consider this. As of early 2018, according to *Forbes* magazine, a mere 2,208 individuals— the world's billionaires—had $9.1 trillion in wealth.[1] If the $9.1 trillion were a foundation endowment with a 5 percent per year payout rate, the annual payout would be $455 billion. That sum could end extreme poverty (SDG 1), ensure universal health coverage (SDG 3), and guarantee access for the poor to a quality education (SDG 4).

Or consider this. According to calculations by the Institute of Economics and Peace, publisher of the Global Peace Index (2017), the global costs of violence in 2016 totaled around $14 trillion (measured at international dollars), or roughly 13 percent of global output. These costs include military and security outlays, the costs of armed conflicts, and the costs of interpersonal violence. While precision in such estimates is difficult, there is no doubt that $14 trillion dwarfs the costs of achieving the Sustainable Development Goals universally, including global energy transformation.

The world's tax havens, small islands like the Cayman Islands and the Virgin Islands, are host to more than $20 trillion of offshore deposits, money that has been moved to these places to avoid taxation and responsibility. In front of our eyes, in broad daylight, these havens of secrecy and unaccountability have been created and nurtured by our own governments, especially the most powerful and richest governments in the world.

This is the challenge of sustainable development: so affordable, so important for well-being, and yet so elusive. If we analyze carefully the realistic path to achieving the SDGs and the Paris Climate Agreement, we find five broad categories of activity that should become the priority work of every government in the world.

First is to ensure quality health and education for all, especially our children, whose entire lives will be shaped by the health care and education we give them in their early years. Without quality health care and education, individuals cannot realistically hope for happy and productive lives. The SDGs include universal commitments to universal health coverage (SDG 3) and universal quality education at least through the secondary level (SDG 4). We have a steep path to success. In many low-income countries, the secondary completion rate today is only 20–30 percent. By 2030, it should be 100 percent.

Second is sustainable land-use management. As I travel the world for the Sustainable Development Goals, I witness in nearly every country that the world is facing a crisis of unsustainable land management, including the loss of biodiversity, soils, freshwater, forest cover, and ecosystem functioning, at rates that are unprecedented and perilous.

Third is decent jobs and infrastructure for all. SDG 1 calls for an end to extreme poverty; SDG 8 aims for decent work for all; and SDGs 6, 7, 9, 11, and 12 include various goals for universal access to infrastructure, including safe water and sanitation, modern energy services including electrification, and transport and communications. Of course, decent work will depend on decent education combined with adequate infrastructure, so the SDGs are interdependent and mutually supportive.

Fourth is to decarbonize the energy system. The shift to zero-carbon energy is the sine qua non of planetary climate safety. By 2050 we have to achieve zero carbon emissions in order to keep global warming within the safety limits set by the Paris Climate Agreement ("well below 2 degrees Celsius" compared with the preindustrial temperature). To achieve this, we will have to be driving electric vehicles rather than cars with internal combustion engines. We will have to be using electricity produced by wind, solar, hydroelectric, geothermal, and other zero-carbon energy sources, rather than by coal, oil, and natural gas. We will have to heat our buildings with electric heat pumps rather than boilers and furnaces. Time is short. Every year we have new evidence that we are at the tipping point of runaway climate disaster.

Fifth is good governance, including honesty, rule of law, fairness, competence, and transparency in managing our politics. Good governance also includes gender equality (SDG 5), reduced inequalities within and among nations (SDG 10), peaceful and inclusive societies (SDG 16), and global cooperation (SDG 17).

THE SDGS AND THE UNITED STATES

Every year the UN Sustainable Development Solutions Network, which I direct on behalf of UN Secretary-General António Guterres, collects data from around the world to assess where countries stand on progress toward the SDGs.[2] The SDG Index gives a global ranking, while the SDG Scorecard highlights the strengths and weaknesses of each of the 150 or so countries for which the requisite global data are available. The SDG Index and Dashboard together therefore offer an objective account of each country's absolute progress toward the goals and its relative position among other nations.

The news is not good for the United States. According to the 2017 SDG Index, the U.S. ranked no better than forty-second out of 157 countries, and thirtieth out of the thirty-five high-income OECD countries. How could the United States, one of the richest countries in the world, rank so low? The reason is clear. The United States is strong on only one of the three pillars of sustainable development, the economy, but weak on social inclusion and environmental sustainability. Inequality is very high in U.S. society, with huge gaps in income and power between men and women, between races, and across educational levels. Environmental sustainability is weak because powerful corporate lobbies for the fossil-fuel and heavy industries have slowed America's transition to low-carbon technologies and primary energy sources.

America pays a very heavy price for its failure to pursue sustainable development. U.S. life expectancy ranks twenty-fifth in the OECD and has actually been declining rather than rising in recent years.[3] The prevalence of clinical depression is up, and the United States has one of the highest rates of depression in the world. Drug addiction and deaths from drug overdoses are soaring. A large part of the U.S. workforce has not gained from economic growth. Confidence in public institutions has plummeted, as has interpersonal trust in American society. For all of these reasons, the self-reported well-being of Americans has also waned.[4]

Compared with other high-income societies, the United States also suffers from chronic violence, thereby falling desperately short of SDG 16, which calls for "peaceful and inclusive societies." America's violence is evident not only in its nonstop overseas wars, but also in its high homicide rates, astounding levels of gun violence, and off-the-chart rates of incarceration, especially of young African-American men. America's violence is also captured by the

2017 Global Peace Index, which placed the United States at the shocking rank of 114th most peaceful country out of the 163 countries measured.[5]

It would not be hard for the United States, with its wealth, skills, and technologies, to achieve the SDGs if it tried to do so. Success would require a change of policies, from corporate tax breaks and environmental deregulation to social programs for the poor and working class and investments in the green economy. Other countries are far ahead of the United States in those directions, and far happier as well.

American consumers have a role to play here. U.S. brand names need to be put on notice: If you cower to the Koch brothers, the American Petroleum Institute, and the Chamber of Commerce, you will pay a price. General Electric, are you with us or against us on saving the planet? How about you, Pepsi, Walmart, IBM, Walt Disney, GM, and other companies whose CEOs have been part of Trump's corporate advisory committees? Responsible consumers need to make clear that they will walk out on brands that are accomplices to Trump's attempts to gut environmental regulations. The Koch brothers spend hundreds of millions of dollars to block action on global warming and pollution, and then have the remarkable audacity to ask Americans to buy consumer products such as AngelSoft and Dixie that they own (via Georgia Pacific–Koch Industries). It's time to say a resounding no!

We must also pressure Congress to act on climate change. Would Republican senators allow the corruption and greed of the Senate to gut the Paris Climate Agreement? It's possible, but these senators have children and grandchildren too, and most are not as stupid as their party's official position on climate change.

THE SDGS AND THE WORLD

Just as is true of the United States, the world as a whole has the human resources, skills, technologies, and wealth to achieve the SDGs. We are, after all, in the midst of one of the most productive and exciting scientific and technological revolutions in history. New digital technologies offer new and better ways to deliver universal health coverage, quality education, equitable finance, low-carbon energy, and improved governance in all parts of the world, even in the poorest and remotest places.

What are the obstacles to surmount? There are several. Corporate lobbies, such as the oil and gas industry, use their power and money to hold back progress. Some of the world's richest people use bribes and campaign contributions to keep their privileges and tax breaks, hoarding funds that should be directed to SDG investments. Irresponsible politicians stoke fear and even war to hold onto power. And governments are too often bereft of practical, workable plans.

There are six main actions we can take to get on track:

First, let us insist that the major companies, especially the fossil-fuel industries, align their business activities with the SDGs.

Second, let us insist that individuals with high net worth should contribute philanthropically to the SDGs, while asset managers should invest their funds according to SDG guidelines.

Third, let us mobilize urgent SDG funding for the world's poorest nations, so that they can provide universal health coverage, universal quality education, and universal access to modern infrastructure.

Fourth, let us insist that war and peace issues be settled according to the UN Charter, especially by the UN Security Council.

Fifth, let us make polluters compensate those who suffer from the pollution, including having the fossil-fuel industries pay for part of the damage caused by global warming.

Sixth, let us deploy breakthroughs in science and technology to achieve more rapid progress toward the SDGs.

In this last regard, the world's universities have an exceptional role to play. As centers of higher education, research, and policy design, universities everywhere should work with governments, businesses, and civil society to help accelerate progress toward the SDGs. The UN Sustainable Development Solutions Network supports hundreds of universities around the world as they step up to support the SDGs.

These are the strategic steps we can take as a global community to achieve the SDGs. As for the United States, one of the most urgent actions is adopting a new foreign policy that will promote sustainable development.

19

A NEW FOREIGN POLICY FOR AMERICAN SECURITY AND WELL-BEING

The purpose of U.S. foreign policy is not to be the mightiest or the most feared or the most powerful nation in the world. It's not to be the richest nation in the world. The purpose of U.S. foreign policy is to achieve national security in a manner that enables Americans to achieve happiness and to help the rest of the world do the same. As I have described, we are far off course. American exceptionalism has proved to be the trap that Ronald Niebuhr so presciently warned against three-quarters of a century ago. America is rich, but it is not safe. It boasts the most billionaires in the world, yet ranks only twenty-fifth among the OECD countries in life expectancy. It is among the most violent parts of the world, ranking 114th in the Global Peace Index, a measure of peaceful societies.

Not every ill can be placed squarely on the illusions of American exceptionalism, but we can say that the endless wars and high costs of military dominance are taking their toll on U.S. society, not to mention the many places caught up in U.S.-caused or U.S.-abetted violence. Corporate lobbying is also a culprit, elevating greed to the top of U.S. politics and leaving well-being far behind. The Sustainable Development Goals, adopted by all countries, including the United States in 2015, but largely ignored by the United States in the Trump era, could help to redirect U.S. domestic and foreign policies toward a more fruitful approach.

I do not expect the Trump administration to pursue the internationalist course that I have recommended. Rather, I believe that the folly of America First will expose itself and cause the nation to redirect its energies and policies. Trump will be gone soon enough. It's our task to prepare a foreign policy for the post-Trump future and to prevent irreparable harms in the meantime.

To summarize the internationalist approach set out in these pages, I conclude with ten priorities for a New American Foreign Policy aimed at achieving true national security and well-being for the American people.

First, live by the UN Charter. The UN remains the world's best hope for peaceful solutions to global problems. There is wisdom in numbers. When the United States faces opposition in the UN Security Council or the UN General Assembly, it should take careful note. More often than not, the opposition is good advice from America's friends, not a plot to subvert U.S. sovereignty.

Second, recommit to the SDGs and the Paris Climate Agreement. The 192 other countries are not wrong. The SDGs and the Paris Climate Agreement are powerful pillars for global economic cooperation in the coming years. By pursuing the SDGs, the United States can start to reverse the plunge in social trust and public health. Together with the rest of the world, the United States can help to avoid devastating climate change, end extreme poverty, and set conditions for peace in today's fragile states.

Third, raise the UN budget. The $600 million that the United States currently spends each year on the regular

UN budget—for the UN General Assembly, UN Security Council, and UN agencies—is the best bargain on the planet. Not only does the United States multiply its own giving roughly five to one, as the other countries add their own assessments, but the UN is the most effective global institution for addressing children's health (UNICEF), epidemic diseases (World Health Organization), famine (World Food Program), refugee movements (UN High Commissioner for Refugees), and much more.

Fourth, ratify the pending UN treaties. After being the original champion and creator of the United Nations, the United States is now the world's loner country. The number of unratified treaties continues to mount, including treaties on women, the disabled, children, the law of the sea, biodiversity, the International Criminal Court, and others. The United States is alone among the 193 UN member states in declaring its intention to withdraw from the Paris Climate Agreement. America's isolation damages America's reputation, weakens global problem solving, and undermines the case for multilateralism.

Fifth, regain momentum on nuclear disarmament. The United States and all other nuclear powers are obligated by the Treaty on the Non-Proliferation of Nuclear Weapons to negotiate in good faith to seek nuclear disarmament. They are not doing so. The International Campaign to Abolish Nuclear Weapons, winner of the 2017 Nobel Peace Prize, and millions of people around the world are pressing for a Treaty on the Prohibition of Nuclear Weapons. These efforts have won the endorsement of 129 countries, including fifty-six signatory states to date. The United States would rekindle global confidence and bolster its own security by championing this new approach rather than spending a trillion dollars to upgrade its nuclear arsenal, as both Obama and Trump have supported.

Sixth, cooperate on new technologies. One key to achieving the SDGs is to advance and implement new technologies in low-carbon energy and transport, smart grids, artificial intelligence, nanotechnologies, genomics, and other sciences. Global cooperation across governments, universities, and business could speed these advances and hasten progress. Transnational technology ventures would build trust and facilitate diffusion of the new technologies around the world.

Seventh, find regional solutions to Middle East violence. The Middle East has suffered a century of violence following the end of World War I because of the chronic meddling of great powers, including Britain, France, Russia, and the United States. The regional powers, notably Iran, Israel, Turkey, and Saudi Arabia, play the big powers against each other. It's time for the UN Security Council to freeze the inflow of armaments and press the regional powers to find a satisfactory framework for mutual security.

Eighth, end the CIA's covert military operations. No institution has done more to undermine America's democracy and to discredit its foreign policy than the CIA when acting in its capacity as the private army of the U.S. president. The CIA routinely violates international law, destabilizes foreign governments, and turns manageable crises into unmanageable disasters, all without public accountability or even awareness. The CIA is necessary and valuable as an intelligence agency; it is a threat to world peace and U.S. security as a secret army.

Ninth, overhaul the U.S. budget. America has starved the portions of federal government that can raise well-being—higher education, job training, family support, environmental conservation, civilian R&D, and sustainable infrastructure—while spending almost a trillion dollars per year on the U.S. military, including hundreds of overseas bases, nonstop overseas conflicts, and hugely expensive weapons systems. With a cooperative foreign policy, the United States could save at least $500 billion per year, which could support vital civilian programs at home while doing far more to help the world's poorest countries end extreme poverty.

Tenth, celebrate America's true exceptionalism. America's exceptionalism does not lie in its military strength, CIA operations, or rejection of UN treaties. America's exceptionalism lies in its cultural and ethnic diversity. New York City, my own home, includes more than 200 nationalities. America's openness to immigrants has brought new energy, ideas, cultural wisdom, and optimism every generation. America's success will depend in no small measure on a foreign policy that champions America as the welcoming home to the world's nations.

Let us therefore enter the Age of Sustainable Development with hope, energy, and determination. This is a time for all countries, especially the major powers, to work cooperatively to raise well-being, protect the environment, end the remnants of extreme poverty, and guard against hatred, fear, and a senseless descent into violence.

ACKNOWLEDGEMENTS

The early drafts of most chapters in this volume originated as a series of op-ed pieces in the *Boston Globe* under the magisterial guidance of editor Marjorie Pritchard. As with the companion volume, *Building the New American Economy*, which also began as *Boston Globe* op-eds, Marjorie has wonderfully edited and encouraged these pieces with an abiding interest in their accuracy, timeliness, and readability. It's wonderful to write under the guidance of a master at the craft!

I'm doubly blessed to have the encouragement, support, and skills of another star editor, Bridget Flannery-McCoy at Columbia University Press. Columbia University Press lives up to its stellar global reputation in every way, and I couldn't be more grateful to be among its authors.

As always, this book has been a family undertaking, with counsel, criticism, pointers, and references coming non-stop from my wife Sonia and our children—and now mentors—Lisa, Adam, and Hannah. I'm grateful that they each undertook repeated readings of the umpteenth draft with fresh eyes and ever-wise suggestions.

ACKNOWLEDGEMENTS

My special assistant Saloni Jain also provided excellent help at all stages of preparing the manuscript.

Finally, I'd like to thank the great truthtellers in our midst, notably Noam Chomsky and Bernie Sanders, for holding America to its promise of equality, the rule of law, and responsibility among the world's nations.

NOTES

INTRODUCTION

1. Henry Luce, "The American Century," *Time*, February 17, 1941.
2. Conrad Cherry, *God's New Israel: Religious Interpretations of American Destiny* (Chapel Hill: University of North Carolina Press, 1998); Stephen M. Walt, "The Myth of American Exceptionalism," *Foreign Policy*, October 11, 2011.
3. Harry S. Stout, "Religion, War, and the Meaning of America," *Religion and American Culture: A Journal of Interpretation* 19, no. 2 (summer 2009): 284.

1. FROM EXCEPTIONALISM TO INTERNATIONALISM

1. President of the United States, *National Security Strategy of the United States of America*, December 2017, https://www.whitehouse.gov/wp-content/uploads/2017/12/NSS-Final-12-18-2017-0905.pdf, 1.
2. Robert D. Blackwill and Ashley J. Tellis, *Revising U.S. Grand Strategy Toward China* (Council Special Report No. 72) (New York: Council on Foreign Relations, March 2015).
3. Blackwill and Tellis, *Revising U.S. Grand Strategy Toward China*, 4.
4. Blackwill and Tellis, *Revising U.S. Grand Strategy Toward China*, 38.

1. FROM EXCEPTIONALISM TO INTERNATIONALISM

5. John F. Kennedy, Commencement Address at American University, June 10, 1963, https://www.jfklibrary.org/Asset -Viewer/BWC7I4C9QUmLG9J6I8oy8w.aspx.
6. Jeffrey D. Sachs, *To Move the World: JFK's Quest for Peace* (New York: Random House, 2013).

2. EXCEPTIONALISM AS THE CIVIC RELIGION

1. Quoted in Reinhold Niebuhr, *The Irony of American History* (New York: Charles Scribner & Sons, 1952), chapter 3. See also Andrew Preston, *Sword of the Spirit, Shield of Faith* (New York: Random House, 2012) for an outstanding account of the role of religion in American wars and foreign policy.
2. John H. Coatsworth, "Liberalism and Big Sticks: The Politics of U.S. Interventions in Latin America, 1898–2004" (Columbia University Academic Commons, 2006), https:// academiccommons.columbia.edu/catalog/ac:204082https:// academiccommons.columbia.edu/catalog/ac:204082.
3. G. J. Meyer, *The World Remade: America in World War I* (New York: Random House, 2016).
4. Henry Luce, "The American Century," *Time*, February 17, 1941.
5. Niebuhr, *The Irony of American History*.
6. Niebuhr, *The Irony of American History*, chapter 3.
7. Niebuhr, *The Irony of American History*, chapter 3.
8. George Kennan, "The Problem of Eastern and Central Europe," *Russia, the Atom, and the West*, BBC Reith Lectures, Lecture 3, November24,1957,http://downloads.bbc.co.uk/rmhttp/radio4 /transcripts/1957_reith3.pdf.
9. Quoted in Joe Conason, " 'Seven Countries in Five Years,' " *Salon*, October 12, 2007, https://www.salon.com/2007/10/12 /wesley_clark/.
10. President of the United States, *National Security Strategy of the United States*, December 2017, https://www.whitehouse.gov /wp-content/uploads/2017/12/NSS-Final-12-18-2017-0905 .pdf.

11. Jeffrey D. Sachs, *Building the New American Economy* (New York: Columbia University Press, 2017).
12. Jeffrey D. Sachs, *The Price of Civilization* (New York: Random House, 2012).

3. THE ERA OF GLOBAL CONVERGENCE

1. Adam Smith, *The Wealth of Nations*, volume 2 (Edinburgh: Doig & Stirling, 1811). The passage cited is from book four, page 488.
2. Charles Kindleberger, *The World in Depression: 1929–1939* (Berkeley: University of California Press, 1986).
3. Francis Fukuyama, "The End of History?" *The National Interest* no. 16 (summer 1989): 3–18.
4. Internet World Stats, 2018, http://www.internetworldstats.com/top20.htm.
5. United Nations, Department of Economic and Social Affairs, Population Division (2017). *World Population Prospects: The 2017 Revision*, DVD Edition. File POP/1-1: Total population (both sexes combined) by region, subregion and country, annually for 1950–2100 (thousands). Medium fertility variant, 2015–2100. https://esa.un.org/unpd/wpp/Download/Standard/Population/.

4. EURASIA ON THE RISE, AMERICA ON THE SIDELINES

1. Jared Diamond, *Guns, Germs, and Steel* (New York: Norton, 2005).
2. People's Republic of China, National Development and Reform Commission (NDRC), "Vision and Actions on Jointly Building Silk Road Economic Belt and 21st-Century Maritime Silk Road," March 28, 2015, http://en.ndrc.gov.cn/newsrelease/201503/t20150330_669367.html.
3. People's Republic of China, "Vision and Actions."

4. EURASIA ON THE RISE, AMERICA ON THE SIDELINES

4. Quoted in Jefferson Chase, "Can Europe Exploit Trump's Protectionism?" *DW News*, January 24, 2017, http://www.dw.com/en/can-europe-exploit-trumps-protectionism/a-37254979.

5. RUSSIA–U.S. RELATIONS IN THE CHANGING WORLD ORDER

1. Jeffrey D. Sachs, *To Move the World: JFK's Quest for Peace* (New York: Random House, 2013).
2. Jeffrey D. Sachs, "Poland's First Economic Reform Plan of July 1989," April 13, 2015, http://jeffsachs.org/2015/04/polands-first-economic-reform-plan-of-july-1989/.; Jeffery D. Sachs, *The End of Poverty* (New York: Penguin, 2005).
3. "Putin's Prepared Remarks at 43rd Munich Conference on Security Policy" [Transcript], February 12, 2007, *Washington Post*, http://www.washingtonpost.com/wp-dyn/content/article/2007/02/12/AR2007021200555.html.

7. ENDING THE ISRAELI-PALESTINIAN CONFLICT

1. Anglo-American Committee of Inquiry, *Report to the United States Government and His Majesty's Government in the United Kingdom*, Lausanne, Switzerland, April 20, 1946 (Washington, DC: Department of State, 1946), http://avalon.law.yale.edu/20th_century/angch01.asp.

8. NORTH KOREA AND THE DOOMSDAY CLOCK

1. *Bulletin of the Atomic Scientists*, "2018 Doomsday Clock Statement." https://thebulletin.org/2018-doomsday-clock-statement.
2. *Bulletin of the Atomic Scientists*, "2018 Doomsday Clock Statement."
3. John F. Kennedy, Commencement Address at American University, Washington, D.C., June 10, 1963, https://www.jfklibrary.org/Research/Research-Aids/JFK-Speeches/American-University_19630610.aspx.

9. TRUMP'S NEW NATIONAL SECURITY STRATEGY

1. President of the United States, *National Security Strategy of the United States of America*, December 2017, https://www.whitehouse.gov/wp-content/uploads/2017/12/NSS-Final-12-18-2017-0905.pdf.

2. U.S. Department of Defense, *Summary of the 2018 National Defense Strategy of the United States of America*, January 2018, https://www.defense.gov/Portals/1/Documents/pubs/2018-National-Defense-Strategy-Summary.pdf.

3. U.S. Department of Defense, *Nuclear Posture Review*, February 2018, https://media.defense.gov/2018/Feb/02/2001872886/-1/-1/1/2018-nuclear-posture-review-final-report.pdf.

4. U.S. Department of Defense, *National Defense Strategy*.

5. President of the United States, *National Security Strategy*.

6. U.S. Department of Defense, *National Defense Strategy*.

7. President of the United States, *National Security Strategy*.

8. Xi Jinping, "Full Text of Xi Jinping's Report at 19th CPC National Congress, October 18, 2017," *China Daily*, November 4, 2017, http://www.chinadaily.com.cn/china/19thcpcnationalcongress/2017-11/04/content_34115212.htm.

9. Xi Jinping, "Report at 19th CPC National Congress."

10. U.S. Department of Defense, *National Defense Strategy*.

11. Gallup, "Rating World Leaders: 2018: The U.S. vs. Germany, China and Russia," downloadable from Politico: https://www.politico.com/f/?id=00000161-0647-da3c-a371-867f6acc0001.

12. Pew Research Center, "U.S. Image Suffers as Publics Around World Question Trump's Leadership: America Still Wins Praise for Its People, Culture and Civil Liberties," June 26, 2017, http://www.pewglobal.org/2017/06/26/u-s-image-suffers-as-publics-around-world-question-trumps-leadership/.

13. David Vine, "Where in the World Is the U.S. Military?" *Politico Magazine*, July/August 2015, https://www.politico.com/magazine/story/2015/06/us-military-bases-around-the-world-119321. See also David Vine, *Base Nation: How U.S.*

Military Bases Abroad Harm America and the World (New York: Metropolitan, 2015).

14. United Nations Office for Disarmament Affairs (UNODA), *Treaty on the Non-Proliferation of Nuclear Weapons (NPT)*, https://www.un.org/disarmament/wmd/nuclear/npt/text/.

15. U.S. Department of Defense, *Nuclear Posture Review*.

16. Military outlays are reported by the Stockholm International Peace Research Institute (SIPRI), using local currency converted to dollars at market exchange rates. I choose the base year 1993 because it is the first year for which SIPRI reports post-Soviet Russia's military outlays. Note that the top-twenty military spenders in 2016 are slightly different from the top-twenty military spenders in 1993. Three countries dropped out of the top-twenty list: Taiwan (province of China), Netherlands, and Sweden. Three others joined the list: Iran, Algeria, and Pakistan. *SIPRI Military Expenditure Database*, https://www.sipri.org/databases/milex.

17. For this calculation, I count as allies in 1993 all NATO countries plus Australia, Israel, Japan, Saudi Arabia, South Korea, Sweden, and Taiwan (province of China), leaving China, India, and Russia as non-allies. As of 2016, I designate six of the top-twenty as non-allies: Algeria, China, India, Iran, Pakistan, and Russia.

10. THE ECONOMIC BALANCE SHEET ON "AMERICA FIRST"

1. Jeffrey D. Sachs, *The Price of Civilization* (New York: Random House, 2012).

2. Jeffrey D. Sachs, *Building the New American Economy* (New York: Columbia University Press, 2017).

3. Sachs, *New American Economy*, especially chapter 7.

4. Bureau of Economic Analysis, U.S. Department of Commerce, "Worldwide Activities of U.S. Multinational Enterprises: Preliminary Results From the 2014 Benchmark Survey," "Table II.G1. Employment of Affiliates, Country by Industry," https://bea.gov/international/usdia2014p.htm, last accessed April 2, 2018.

13. WILL TRUMP HAND CHINA THE TECHNOLOGICAL LEAD?

1. National Academy of Sciences, *Rising Above the Gathering Storm* (Washington, DC: National Academies Press, 2007).

15. FROM DIPLOMATIC LEADER TO ROGUE NATION

1. Pew Research Center, "Favorable Views of the UN Prevail in Europe, Asia and U.S." September 20, 2016, http://www.pewresearch.org/fact-tank/2016/09/20/favorable-views-of-the-un-prevail-in-europe-asia-and-u-s/.
2. Nikki Haley, "Remarks Before a UN General Assembly Vote on Jerusalem," December 21, 2017, https://usun.state.gov/remarks/8232.
3. "Turkey Says U.N. Jerusalem Vote Showed Dignity, Sovereignty 'Not for Sale,'" *Reuters*, December 21, 2017, https://www.reuters.com/article/us-usa-trump-israel-un-turkey/turkey-says-u-n-jerusalem-vote-showed-dignity-sovereignty-not-for-sale-idUSKBN1EF2HJ.

16. THE ETHICS AND PRACTICALITIES OF FOREIGN AID

1. Letter to congressional leaders Ryan, Pelosi, McConnell, and Schumer, February 27, 2017, http://www.usglc.org/downloads/2017/02/FY18_International_Affairs_Budget_House_Senate.pdf.

17. MANAGING MIGRATION

1. "Trump's Speech to Congress," *New York Times*, February 28, 2017, https://www.nytimes.com/2017/02/28/us/politics/trump-congress-video-transcript.html.
2. Pew Research Center, "Public Remains Conflicted Over Islam," August 24, 2010, http://www.pewforum.org/2010/08/24/public-remains-conflicted-over-islam.

3. James Q. Whitman, *Hitler's American Model: The United States and the Making of Nazi Race Law* (Princeton, NJ: Princeton University Press, 2017), 45–46.

18. ACHIEVING SUSTAINABLE DEVELOPMENT

1. Kerry A. Dolan and Luisa Kroll, "Forbes Billionaires 2018: Meet The Richest People On The Planet," *Forbes*, March 6, 2018, https://www.forbes.com/sites/luisakroll/2018/03/06/forbes-billionaires-2018-meet-the-richest-people-on-the-planet/#57465ba56523
2. Sustainable Development Solutions Network, SDG Index and Dashboards Report 2017, http://sdgindex.org/.
3. John Helliwell, Richard Layard, and Jeffrey Sachs, eds., *World Happiness Report 2018* (New York: Sustainable Development Solutions Network, 2018).
4. John Helliwell, Richard Layard, and Jeffrey Sachs, eds., *World Happiness Report 2017* (New York: Sustainable Development Solutions Network, 2017).
5. Institute for Economics and Peace, *Global Peace Index 2017*, http://visionofhumanity.org/app/uploads/2017/06/GPI17-Report.pdf.

REFERENCES

Anglo-American Committee of Inquiry. *Report to the United States Government and His Majesty's Government in the United Kingdom.* Lausanne, Switzerland, April 20, 1946. Washington, DC: Department of State, 1946. http://avalon.law.yale.edu/20th_century/angcho1.asp.

Blackwill, Robert D., and Ashley J. Tellis. *Revising U.S. Grand Strategy Toward China* (Council Special Report No. 72). New York: Council on Foreign Relations, March 2015.

Bulletin of the Atomic Scientists, Science and Security Board. "2018 Doomsday Clock Statement." January 25, 2018. https://thebulletin.org/2018-doomsday-clock-statement.

Bush, Vannevar. *Science: The Endless Frontier.* Washington, DC: U.S. Government Printing Office, 1945.

Chase, Jefferson. "Can Europe Exploit Trump's Protectionism?" *DW News*, January 24, 2017. http://www.dw.com/en/can-europe-exploit-trumps-protectionism/a-37254979.

Cherry, Conrad. *God's New Israel: Religious Interpretations of American Destiny.* Chapel Hill: University of North Carolina Press, 1998.

Coatsworth, John H. "Liberalism and Big Sticks: The Politics of U.S. Interventions in Latin America, 1898–2004." Columbia University Academic Commons, 2006. https://academiccommons.columbia.edu/catalog/ac:204082.

Conason, Joe. " 'Seven Countries in Five Years.' " *Salon*, October 12, 2007. https://www.salon.com/2007/10/12/wesley_clark/.

Diamond, Jared. *Guns, Germs, and Steel.* New York: Norton, 2005.

REFERENCES

"Doomsday Clock." *Wikipedia*. https://en.wikipedia.org/wiki/Doomsday_Clock.

"Enlargement of NATO," *Wikipedia*, https://en.wikipedia.org/wiki/Enlargement_of_NATO.

Fukuyama, Francis. "The End of History?" *The National Interest* no. 16 (summer 1989): 3–18.

Global Fund. *Results Report 2017*. https://www.theglobalfund.org/media/6773/corporate_2017resultsreport_report_en.pdf.

Haley, Nikki. "Remarks Before a UN General Assembly Vote on Jerusalem," December 21, 2017. https://usun.state.gov/remarks/8232.

Helliwell, John, Richard Layard, and Jeffrey Sachs, eds. *World Happiness Report 2017*. New York: Sustainable Development Solutions Network, 2017.

——. *World Happiness Report 2018*. New York: Sustainable Development Solutions Network, 2018.

Institute for Economics and Peace. *Global Peace Index 2017*. http://visionofhumanity.org/app/uploads/2017/06/GPI17-Report.pdf.

Kennan, George. "The Problem of Eastern and Central Europe." *Russia, the Atom, and the West*. BBC Reith Lectures, Lecture 3, November 24, 1957. http://downloads.bbc.co.uk/rmhttp/radio4/transcripts/1957_reith3.pdf.

Kennedy, John F. Commencement Address at American University, Washington, D.C., June 10, 1963. https://www.jfklibrary.org/Research/Research-Aids/JFK-Speeches/American-University_19630610.aspx.

——. Inaugural Address. January 20, 1961. http://avalon.law.yale.edu/20th_century/kennedy.asp.

Kindleberger, Charles. *The World in Depression: 1929–1939*. Berkeley: University of California Press, 1986.

Maddison, Angus. Maddison Project Database, version 2010, https://www.rug.nl/ggdc/historicaldevelopment/maddison/releases/maddison-database-2010.

Meyer, G. J. *The World Remade: America in World War I*. New York: Random House, 2016.

National Academy of Sciences. *Rising Above the Gathering Storm*. Washington, DC: National Academies Press, 2007.

Niebuhr, Reinhold. *The Irony of American History*. New York: Charles Scribner & Sons, 1952.

Organization for Economic Cooperation and Development (OECD). "Development Aid Rises Again in 2016." April 11, 2017. https://www.oecd.org/dac/financing-sustainable-development/development-finance-data/ODA-2016-detailed-summary.pdf.

People's Republic of China, National Development and Reform Commission (NDRC). "Vision and Actions on Jointly Building Silk Road Economic Belt and 21st-Century Maritime Silk Road." March 28, 2015. http://en.ndrc.gov.cn/newsrelease/201503/t20150330_669367.html.

Pope Paul VI. "*Populorum Progressio*: Encyclical on the Development of Peoples." March 26, 1967. http://w2.vatican.va/content/paul-vi/en/encyclicals/documents/hf_p-vi_enc_26031967_populorum.html.

President of the United States. *National Security Strategy of the United States of America*. December 2017. https://www.whitehouse.gov/wp-content/uploads/2017/12/NSS-Final-12-18-2017-0905.pdf.

Preston, Andrew. *Sword of the Spirit, Shield of Faith*. New York: Random House, 2012.

"Putin's Prepared Remarks at 43rd Munich Conference on Security Policy" [Transcript], February 12, 2007, *Washington Post*, http://www.washingtonpost.com/wp-dyn/content/article/2007/02/12/AR2007021200555.html.

Sachs, Jeffrey D. *Building the New American Economy*. New York: Columbia University Press, 2017.

——. *The End of Poverty*. New York: Penguin, 2005.

——. *The Price of Civilization*. New York: Random House, 2012.

——. *To Move the World: JFK's Quest for Peace*. New York: Random House, 2013.

Stout, Harry S. "Religion, War, and the Meaning of America." *Religion and American Culture: A Journal of Interpretation* 19, no. 2 (summer 2009): 275–89.

Sustainable Development Solutions Network. SDG Index and Dashboards Report 2017. http://sdgindex.org/.

REFERENCES

"Trump's Speech to Congress." *New York Times*, February 28, 2017. https://www.nytimes.com/2017/02/28/us/politics/trump-congress-video-transcript.html.

"Turkey Says U.N. Jerusalem Vote Showed Dignity, Sovereignty 'Not for Sale.'" *Reuters*, December 21, 2017. https://www.reuters.com/article/us-usa-trump-israel-un-turkey/turkey-says-u-n-jerusalem-vote-showed-dignity-sovereignty-not-for-sale-idUSKBN1EF2HJ.

United Nations, Department of Economic and Social Affairs, Population Division. *World Population Prospects: The 2017 Revision*, Volume I: Comprehensive Tables. 2017. https://esa.un.org/unpd/wpp/publications/Files/WPP2017_Volume-I_Comprehensive-Tables.pdf.

United Nations Office for Disarmament Affairs (UNODA). *Treaty on the Non-Proliferation of Nuclear Weapons (NPT)*. https://www.un.org/disarmament/wmd/nuclear/npt/text/.

U.S. Department of Defense. *Nuclear Posture Review*. February 2018. https://media.defense.gov/2018/Feb/02/2001872886/-1/-1/1/2018-nuclear-posture-review-final-report.pdf.

——. *Summary of the 2018 National Defense Strategy of the United States of America*. January 2018. https://www.defense.gov/Portals/1/Documents/pubs/2018-National-Defense-Strategy-Summary.pdf.

Vine, David. *Base Nation: How U.S. Military Bases Abroad Harm America and the World*. New York: Metropolitan Books, 2015.

——. "Where in the World Is the U.S. Military?" *Politico Magazine*, July/August 2015. https://www.politico.com/magazine/story/2015/06/us-military-bases-around-the-world-119321.

Walt, Stephen M. "The Myth of American Exceptionalism." *Foreign Policy*, October 11, 2011.

Wan, Haibin. *Connotation of Global Energy Interconnection and Asian Grid Interconnection*. Global Energy Interconnection Development and Cooperation Organization, September 2016. https://www.renewable-ei.org/images/pdf/20160908/Wan_Haibin_GlobalEnergy Interconnections.pdf.

Whitman, James Q. *Hitler's American Model: The United States and the Making of Nazi Race Law*. Princeton, NJ: Princeton University Press, 2017.

REFERENCES

Xi Jinping. "Full Text of Xi Jinping's Report at 19th CPC National Congress, October 18, 2017." *China Daily*, November 4, 2017. http://www.chinadaily.com.cn/china/19thcpcnationalcongress /2017-11/04/content_34115212.htm.

INDEX